T0267948

Praise for *Married into the Family*

What an incredibly needed book! Whether you have a great relationship with your in-laws or a challenging one, you have to read this book. Our friends Dave and Ashley Willis provide the practical wisdom and biblical encouragement all of us need for this important area of marriage.

Shaunti and Jeff Feldhahn
Social Researchers
Bestselling authors of *For Women Only* and *For Men Only*

Dave and Ashley address the elephant in the room every couple faces but few want to deal with. *Married into the Family* is your how-to guide to help you navigate the highly sensitive and awkward conversations couples must learn to have with each other and with both sides of the family so they can live guilt free and thrive no matter the circumstances.

Rodney and Michelle Gage
Authors of *Family Shift*
Founders of *The Winning Family*

Dave and Ashley Willis have done it again! They took a tough and often complicated topic and broke it down into simple actions in an authentic, biblical, and practical way. *Married into the Family: The Not-so-Secret Guide to In-Law Relationship* is a must-read for everyone, from newlyweds to those who have been married for decades. This is a resource I will be recommending to all of my counseling clients.

Rachael Gilbert, MMFT
Owner of BBC Health, Host of *Real Talk with Rachael* Podcast
Author of *Image Restored*

If I could, I would apologize to the hundreds of couples I have done premarital counseling with and not shared this resource with them. My only consolation is that it wasn't available until now! In-law relationships are one of the leading causes of marital stress, and going forward, I will be recommending this book to Thanks to Dave and Ashley for this valuable resource.

Ron Edmondson
Pastor and Podcaster
Author of *The Mythical Leader*

Dave and Ashley discuss a difficult topic in such an easy to approach manner. The stories are relatable and applicable, regardless of the situation you find yourself in. This is a phenomenal resource combining biblical truth, clinical application, and self-reflection questions that are bound to lead to a deeper level of healing. I'm so thankful for this couple and their ability to discuss the hard topics in marriage today.

Cassie Reid, Ph.D., LPC-Supervisor
Director of Marriage and Family Therapy
Associate Professor of Counseling, The King's University

When two rivers come together, it's bound to get turbulent. Marriage is like two rivers coming together, and in-laws are one of those powerful upstream forces in that new current. I love how Dave and Ashley keep it real in this book and help us see how to courageously and graciously navigate those turbulent waters of relationships with in-laws. This book is a gift that offers hope for your marriage.

Joël Malm
Counselor and Author of *Connecting the Dots*

It's the ultimate guide for couples wanting to create unbreakable bonds and healthy boundaries with their extended family. Full of powerful insights and easy-to-follow advice, Dave and Ashley's empathetic approach makes you feel like you're sitting down with trusted friends. If you're longing for harmony and deep connections with your in-laws, don't miss out on this life-changing book.

Bob & Linda Lotich
Authors of *Simple Money, Rich Life*
Hosts of *SeedTime Money* Podcast

There are few people in the world who have the passion, knowledge, and experience that Dave and Ashley Willis bring to the table when it comes to marriage ministry. I am honored to call them friends, and I am excited to endorse their latest book, *Married into the Family*. Managing the in-laws in marriage is something that is rarely discussed but drastically needed. Dave and Ashley get surgical in this book and bring a deep yet simple-to-follow guide that I know will bless you as much as it did Michele and me.

Dr. Jon Chasteen
Lead Pastor of Victory Church

In-laws ... if you know, you know! Dave and Ashley look into an issue many marriages are trying to navigate. This insightful, honest, and practical book will encourage you and equip you to navigate the subject of in-laws with clear biblical truth and real-life examples. This book is an excellent tool to help you lean into the tension of your feelings about this subject and what God has said.

Beau and Olivia Guidry
Director of Small Groups, First Moss Bluff Church

MARRIED INTO THE FAMILY

THE NOT-SO-SECRET GUIDE TO *IN-LAW RELATIONSHIPS*

Dave & Ashley Willis

Married into the Family: The Not-So-Secret Guide to In-Law Relationships
Copyright © 2023 by Dave and Ashley Willis

Unless otherwise indicated, all Scripture quotations are taken from the Holy Bible, New Living Translation, copyright © 1996, 2004, 2015 by Tyndale House Foundation. Used by permission of Tyndale House Publishers, Carol Stream, Illinois 60188. All rights reserved.

Scripture quotations marked (ESV) are taken from the ESV® Bible (The Holy Bible, English Standard Version®), copyright © 2001 by Crossway, a publishing ministry of Good News Publishers. Used by permission. All rights reserved. The ESV text may not be quoted in any publication made available to the public by a Creative Commons license. The ESV may not be translated in whole or in part into any other language.

Scripture quotations marked (NIV) are taken from the Holy Bible, New International Version®, NIV®. Copyright © 1973, 1978, 1984, 2011 by Biblica, Inc.™ Used by permission of Zondervan. All rights reserved worldwide. www.zondervan.com. The "NIV" and "New International Version" are trademarks registered in the United States Patent and Trademark Office by Biblica, Inc.™

Scripture quotations marked (NKJV) are taken from the New King James Version®. Copyright © 1982 by Thomas Nelson. Used by permission. All rights reserved.

All rights reserved. No portion of this publication may be reproduced, stored in a retrieval system, or transmitted in any form by any means—electronic, mechanical, photocopying, recording, or any other—without prior permission from the publisher. "XO Marriage" is a trademark registered in the United States Patent and Trademark Office by XO Marriage.

ISBN: 978-0-9600831-3-8 Paperback
ISBN: 978-0-9600831-8-3 eBook
ISBN: 978-0-9600831-9-0 audiobook

XO Publishing is a leading creator of relationship-based resources. We focus primarily on marriage-related content for churches, small group curriculum, and people looking for timeless truths about relationships and overall marital health. For more information on other resources from XO Publishing, visit XOMarriage.com.

XO Marriage®, an imprint of XO Publishing
1021 Grace Lane
Southlake, TX 76092

While the authors make every effort to provide accurate URLs at the time of printing for external or third-party Internet websites, neither they nor the publisher assume any responsibility for changes or errors made after publication.

Printed in the United States of America

23 24 25 26—5 4 3 2 1

Contents

Section Three: Special Cases

Section Four: Legacy

Acknowledgments

So many people have had an impact on our story and helped give life to this book. Even before we mention these important friends, colleagues, and mentors who have shaped this book, we want to thank *you* for taking the time to read it. By reading, applying, and sharing the message of this book, you have joined with us in building healthier lives and healthier marriages. Thank you!

- We want to thank our own in-laws for their lifelong love and support. Bill and Mary McCray and Brad and Karen Willis have loved us well and done much good in creating a thriving, multigenerational family. We invite you to go to YouTube and watch our interviews with each of these extraordinary couples on our *Naked Marriage* Podcast. You can search for the episodes titled "Ashley's Parents" and "Dave's Parents." They share some amazing wisdom plus some hilarious stories too!

- Speaking of family, we also want to thank our siblings and our extended family for all you do for us. We have been blessed with some amazing relatives! Special thanks to our precious sons Cooper, Connor, Chandler, and Chatham. We love you boys, and all we do we do for you. The greatest honor in our lives is the privilege of being your parents. We promise to do our best to be there for you through every part of life and to be the best in-laws possible to your future wives. We cannot wait to welcome them into our family someday!

- Our deepest gratitude and appreciation go to XO Marriage President Brent Evans. His leadership and ongoing support make all our work at XO Marriage possible. We are truly honored to call the entire Evans family our friends, and we are equally honored that they've adopted us into the XO Marriage family.

- We are deeply humbled and grateful to collaborate with an incredible team at XO Marriage. This book may have our names on the front, but like every aspect of this ministry, it was truly a team effort. We have the privilege of serving as part of a world-class team of people who serve and lead wholeheartedly with authentic faith, tenacious grit, and contagious enthusiasm. We want to thank the XO Publishing team for their extraordinary work in shaping this book. The team includes Daniel Van, Karina Lopez, Dr. John Andersen, Kathy Krenzien, and Jenny Morgan.

- We extend our heartfelt gratitude to our church family at Stevens Creek Church in Augusta, Georgia. The staff and community at "The Creek" have been a constant source of encouragement and support for our family in ways we could never repay. We love our church!

- Our heartfelt gratitude also extends to our friends near and far who have helped shape the content of this book through your stories, encouragement, and prayers. For those social media friends and the Naked Marriage Podcast listeners whom we have never met in person but have encouraged us, prayed for us, and shared our content with others, please know that your impact on this ministry and in our lives is profound. Thank you for your partnership in this work of building healthier marriages and pointing more people to God's love, grace, and peace.

- Finally, and most importantly, we want to thank Jesus Christ, our Lord and Savior. He is the Giver of all good things. True health in life, in faith, and in marriage is only possible because of Him.

Introduction

Why Does It Have to Be So Complicated?

Relationships with in-laws are some of the most complicated and consequential connections we will ever know. We want to promote health and healing in our families because it is important, but it isn't always easy. The way we treat the in-law relationship when we marry into a new family is going to have a significant impact on the rest of our lives and even on the legacy we leave behind.

If you have picked up this book because you are engaged and preparing to marry, then we say *congratulations!* You are making a wise choice right at the start of your life together as you invest in healthy relationships with your immediate and extended families.

If you have an adult child who has become engaged or recently married, and you are trying to navigate these unfamiliar waters, then it's an exciting time, but it might also be complicated. We want you to know you are making an excellent choice to read this book. We hope it will bless you and your entire family.

We recognize that some people will seek out or be offered this book because their family is in a state of crisis. If that describes your situation, then we know there's frustration, miscommunication, brokenness, and even feelings of hopelessness. We are glad you have found this book. No situation is ever completely hopeless, and you are never alone in your suffering and confusion. As we write this, we are praying this book will help you to feel seen and heard. We are asking God to use the principles you will find here to encourage you and give you practical steps to build (or rebuild) your relationships.

In our work at XO Marriage, we receive messages every day from people looking for help navigating their in-law relationships. One of the biggest inspirations for why we chose to write this book comes from those who have reached out to us. Recently we received this message:

> *Dave and Ashley,*
>
> *Please HELP! My marriage is in crisis, and my wife won't even admit there is a problem. It has to do with my mother-in-law (MIL). My wife was always very close to her mom, which on the surface seems like a good thing, but their relationship seems really out-of-balance to me. Once I came into the picture, my mother-in-law seemed threatened by me because I was "stealing" her daughter away, and she expected to have 24/7 access to my wife. There's only peace in our home when I don't do anything to disrupt my MIL's plans with my wife. From my perspective, my wife's parents have never had a great marriage, so my wife's mom has always leaned on my wife for spouse-level friendship and emotional support. They have a codependent relationship in which even now my wife feels like she needs her mom's permission and approval for our decisions.*
>
> *My wife has been in this dynamic so long it does not even seem weird or unhealthy to her. I try to tell her that it is not normal or healthy to be constantly available to her mom, but she replies that she's just "honoring her parents" like it says to do in the Bible. That "honor your parents" Bible verse seems to be the only one my MIL likes to quote, and she quotes it often. I could go on and on with more examples of how my MIL has gaslighted, sabotaged, manipulated, punished, and controlled my wife. I feel trapped. I feel like there is no room for me in my own marriage unless I play by my MIL's twisted rules. It is like my wife is married to her mom, and I'm just the roommate. I can't go on like this, but*

I have no idea how to change the situation or even convince my wife that there is a real problem. What do I do???

We feel the heartbreaking desperation in this husband's plea. He longs for a deep and intimate connection with his wife, but it is currently being disrupted by an outside force. His wife does not see the problem in the same way a fish doesn't realize it's wet. Water is the only world a fish has ever known, just like dysfunction is all this wife has ever known in her relationship with her mom. Human minds can become trained and conditioned to see any form of dysfunction as "normal" if it happens long enough without being challenged.

The Bible clearly says God's plan for marriage requires a man and woman to leave their families of origin and join as a new family (see Genesis 2:24). Outside of our relationship with God, the one we have with our spouse is the most important relationship we will know on earth. No other human relationship, including the ones we have with our parents or children, can replace the priority God puts on the married couple. When the marriage relationship comes first, then all other family relationships will find health and balance. When we replace a marriage relationship with anything else, then all relationships and our own mental health will eventually suffer from it.

A healthy in-law experience is one of life's greatest blessings, but an unhealthy connection is one of life's most difficult challenges. Depending on your in-laws' unique personalities and your own, these difficulties might have countless unpredictable or unpleasant ramifications. In-law dynamics can become your primary source of marital conflict and stress. These relationships might also reveal some of the most unhealthy parts of yourself, which can make recapturing healthy relationships even more complicated. We recognize it is likely you're experiencing some negativity in your in-law relationships right now, which is why you're reading this book. We want you to find answers, encouragement, and perspectives in what we have written here. We hope it will help you build bridges toward healing with your in-laws. Our greatest desire is for more health and unity in your marriage. We wrote this book for *you*.

Even if your in-laws are causing stress and strain in your marriage, we encourage you to resist the urge to view them as your "enemy." Most of the time, overbearing in-laws are not consciously trying to harm or sabotage you or your marriage. They are simply acting out the same broken family dynamics that they experienced and perpetuated themselves through the years. Their motives usually come from a desire to remain close to their children, thinking they are steering their kids' lives in the "right" direction. Nevertheless, when their actions, regardless of their motives, start to create conflict in your home, then you must respond appropriately.

Even as you take the actions outlined in this book and put healthy boundaries or ground rules in place, always remember to act with compassion and empathy. If you keep that attitude, then your own heart will not grow bitter. You will also create space for a healthier relationship with your in-laws in the future, which is a major goal of this book. We must tell you that the aim of this book is not to help you create a plan to completely remove your in-laws from your life. Instead, we want to walk with you and help you create an atmosphere of mutual respect in which you and your in-laws can see each other as a gift. Some extreme circumstances may make it necessary for you to distance yourself temporarily or permanently from your in-laws, and in some rare cases, you may need to cut off all contact with some family members. However, that action should be a last resort after every other option has been exhausted.

Before we dive into rest of the book, we want to give a few explanations and disclaimers. First, we love our in-laws! Seriously, both sets of our parents and extended families are a source of great encouragement for us. We even vacation with our families and cherish our time together with them. We have tons of fun. Some of our greatest memories are those we have made together with family. We know God has blessed us through them, but over the years there have been times when some of these relationships were strained. We know what it is like to deal with an enormous amount of stress in these relationships. In fact, several years ago, many of our marriage's darkest days resulted from these family relationships.

If you are reading this book because of a damaged or unhealthy relationship with one or more in-law, then please understand that we can relate to and empathize with your experience. We have seen God do great miracles in our own families through the years, but we all continue to be works-in-progress. In this book we will share what we have learned from our own personal experiences, but we will use discretion. In celebration of how far we have come in our own family relationships and to show respect and protect everyone involved, we won't share specifics about negative experiences within our own families, and we won't use any actual names.

That being said, every account you will read in this book has an actual, true story at its roots. We have changed some details, but again, that is to protect the people we care about. These stories stand for real people and real situations. Some stories we share come from people we have counseled either in person or online. Just as we did with our own family, we have altered some details to protect the identities of those involved. With that said, the principles these stories illustrate remain true and tested, and you can confidently apply them to your own situation.

Second, when we use the term *in-laws,* we are referring broadly to the multi-generational families connected to you and your spouse. You can think of your in-laws as your spouse's family or as the younger generation once your own children start getting married. We hope this book will help you build strong bonds with all those relatives and that it will equip you with new strategies to build more unity across your entire family. We pray you will become the heathiest in-law you can be to your spouse's parents, their siblings, your children's spouses, and every other family member with whom you relate.

We share illustrations that relate to parents, siblings, kids, grandkids, and blended families, but our primary focus is on the relationship you and your spouse have with your parents and with your spouse's parents. We have chosen to concentrate on this particular relationship because it seems to set the tone for all other family relationships.

Finally, while we draw on social research, personal experience, and the experiences of others, our primary source of authority for this book is the Bible. As followers of Jesus, we believe God's heart is for all of us to experience healing and wholeness in our relationship with Him and our relationships with each other. God's Word gives us the only reliable blueprint for how these relationships can be successful. We do not quote Scripture in every paragraph, but God outlines His perfect plan for relationships in the Bible, and it has shaped every part of this book.

Even if you are not (yet) a Christian, please don't discount or toss aside this book. You will be amazed at the relevance and timeless wisdom the Bible gives to help us navigate our relationships. We wholeheartedly believe you are not reading this book by accident. God has a beautiful plan to reconcile and renew your family. All families are imperfect, but while they can be messy, they can also be a source of great blessing.

Your family may have gone through innumerable cycles of generational brokenness and dysfunction, but that does not have to define you or your marriage! With God's help, you can author a new story. You have the power to break the chain. You can create a new and better legacy for your children and for future generations.

We want you to believe there are blessings in store for your family. By reading this book and applying what you learn, you are making a powerful investment in your family's future. We are honored to be on this journey with you.

Before we go any further, it is important for you to assess where you and your spouse are at this point. Take a moment with your spouse and discuss the following questions:

1. If you could change anything about your relationship with your in-laws, what would it be? Why did you choose that answer?

2. Do you believe you can make the necessary changes? Why or why not?

3. Do you feel like your spouse understands why you feel the way you do about your in-laws? If the answer is no, then share your point of view with your spouse.

Let's pray:

Heavenly Father, we come to You today as a united couple who wants to have a strong marriage and a healthy relationship with our family and in-laws. At this point, things are not where they need to be, but we know that all things are possible with You. Help us approach this journey with humility, positivity, honesty, and vulnerability. We surrender ourselves, our marriage, and our families to You, Lord. In Jesus' name, Amen.

SECTION ONE

LEAVE & CLEAVE

This explains why a man leaves his father and mother and is joined to his wife, and the two are united into one.

—Genesis 2:24

My husband wasn't fully committed to me in the early years of our marriage. There was another woman more important to him. His "unfaithfulness" to me wasn't the result of a mistress or any sexual form of infidelity. He was more committed to his mother's happiness than his wife's happiness. He wanted his parents to see him more as a good son than as a good husband. It was a frustrating season, but eventually, he came to see God's design for marriage and began to put me first. Now, we have a great marriage. Ironically, he even has a much healthier relationship with his mom now that clearer boundaries are in place. We almost didn't survive those early years. Until a couple truly learns what it means to "leave and cleave," they'll never experience true intimacy or oneness in their marriage.

—Maggie P. (Married 22 years)

CHAPTER 1

God Speaks About In-Laws

You probably have heard this quote: "When you marry your spouse, you also marry their family." When you first heard it, it might have sounded strange and far-fetched, because until you got married, your main connection to your spouse's family was *your spouse.* You might have had a glimpse of your spouse's family, but now you have an eyeful. Now you know there is a lot of truth to that statement.

When you married your spouse, you told the world you committed your life to them, but you simultaneously made a pledge to your spouse's family. If you did not realize what that meant at the time, then you're not alone. Obviously, your commitment to your spouse's family is at a different level than the one you made to your spouse, but nonetheless those family commitments are real. You will have an ongoing relationship with your in-laws, and that is why you will need boundaries and ground rules, which we will discuss throughout this book.

The Bible has a lot to say about every important relationship in life, including our relationships with in-laws. It is important for us to attend to the sacred importance of loving and respecting our in-laws. Our expression of love and respect is something God honors. In His perfect wisdom, He does not always reveal His lessons and principles in a list of bullet points. God often tells us stories and uses them to illuminate the truth. The Bible's story of Ruth and Naomi is one of the clearest and most compelling examples of the ways in-law relationships can be sources of great blessings.

If you have attended many weddings, then there's a good chance you've heard a reading from the book of Ruth. You might have even chosen a selection of the book for someone to read at your own wedding. Ruth's words to her mother-in-law are some of the Bible's most beautiful verses. They show the power and beauty of real commitment.

> But Ruth replied, "Don't ask me to leave you and turn back. Wherever you go, I will go; wherever you live, I will live. Your people will be my people, and your God will be my God. Wherever you die, I will die, and there I will be buried. May the LORD punish me severely if I allow anything but death to separate us!" (Ruth 1:16–17).

Ruth's words, spoken in a time of crisis, beautifully capture the commitment necessary for a strong marriage, but ironically, these words were not delivered in the context of marriage at all. In fact, Ruth's mother-in-law heard her magnificent promise spoken in a very unexpected way. This account provides us with some of the Bible's most fascinating insights into God's plan for in-law relationships.

Ruth lived about 3,000 years ago. She was a young woman from the land of Moab, which was about 50 miles from her mother-in-law's hometown. That may seem like a short distance, but for two women traveling alone, it would have been several days' journey accompanied by untold danger. In fact, times were exceedingly difficult back then, especially after Ruth's young husband died. Based on the religious and cultural customs of the day, Ruth no longer had any obligation to her husband's family once he died. She was free to pursue a new life as she saw fit. But even though Ruth could do as she wished, she refused to leave her mother-in-law, Naomi.

Ruth knew Naomi had no one, so she selflessly committed her life to her mother-in-law's service. Because of Ruth's selflessness, God blessed her in remarkable ways. Not only did God supply food, shelter, and safety for the two women, but He also brought a man named Boaz into Ruth's life.

Boaz[1], a wealthy kinsman redeemer[2], married Ruth, and together they started a family. Their lineage became a world-changing generational legacy. Ruth and Boaz had a son named Obed who had a son named Jesse who had a son named David. David became the greatest king in Israel's history and the author of many of the Bible's psalms and poems.

King David's lineage continued with his son Solomon, who wrote much of the Bible's wisdom literature. God blessed King Solomon to become the wisest man who ever lived except for Jesus. However, all this royalty, wisdom, and wealth were only the tip of the iceberg. God's ultimate plan through Ruth and Boaz's family tree would happen a thousand years later.

A young Jewish couple made their way to Bethlehem, the City of David, for a government-mandated census. The young woman, Mary, was expecting a child. She would give birth to a son and name Him Jesus. He was and is the Son of God. He was and is the Prince of Peace. He was and is the embodiment of love. He is also a descendant of King David (see Matthew 1:6–16; Luke 1:69).

God brought His own Son through the lineage of a poor young widow named Ruth. She understood the power of commitment and the meaning of love. God wants to create a generational impact through your life as well. The level at which God measures your eternal impact will be the level of your commitment to the people He has placed in your life.

> The level at which God measures your
> eternal impact will be the level of your
> commitment to the people
> He has placed in your life.

Ruth had no way of knowing how the world would change as a direct result of her love and selfless commitment to her mother-in-law. God honored her devotion and blessed her. He also blessed the world through her. We will unpack this story in more detail later, but for now, we want to emphasize that God has given each of us the opportunity to receive this blessing. He also wants us to be a blessing to others when we choose to love them. In our lifetime, we will not see the full manifestation of this blessing, but we can be sure God will continue the blessing to and through our descendants because of the love we give.

Honoring parents (yours and your spouse's)

Ruth is a powerful example of honoring and respecting an in-law. For some, giving respect to their or their spouse's parents feels impossible, but God will always honor us when we honor our parents. We say this with an important disclaimer: honoring your parents or in-laws does not mean obeying their every wish, nor does it require you to subject yourself to abusive behaviors, which we will discuss later.

Honoring simply means giving respect for the position in which God has placed your parents and in-laws and for the good they have done. It requires the choice to focus on the good rather than the bad. Only our heavenly Father is perfect, and no earthly parent can rise to God's level of perfection. Even so, every parent deserves respect despite their inherent imperfections. As we give them our lifelong honor and respect, we are putting wisdom into action and securing multi-generational blessings.

There are *two principles that will help us show honor to our parents and our in-laws:*

The first principle is to honor our parents by *living in honor and integrity ourselves.* When we choose to embody the positive lessons they taught us, they experience a rich blessing and the fulfillment of the dreams and prayers they've had for us since we were born. You simultaneously honor your parents and honor God by choosing to live a life of integrity, wisdom, and honor.

A second principle is to honor our parents and in-laws *by forgiving them.* Parents and in-laws are not perfect. (Remember, only God can have perfection.) There were times your parents or in-laws made mistakes, which may have caused you great pain. Forgiveness does not excuse sin, but it does place those past wounds in God's hands, making healing possible in your heart and in your relationships with those who hurt you. If it's within your power to rebuild a broken bridge, then *you* be the one to start by extending grace. As you do, you will be walking the path of wisdom and peace. Even if a parent has been absent all your life, instead of allowing bitterness or insecurity to take root in your heart, choose to lean into the loving presence of your heavenly Father who has never left your side.

When you extend this kind of grace to the generation ahead of you, it will set a powerful example for the generations behind you. It will equip your children with the tools to follow in your footsteps by giving honor and respect to you once they are grown and have spouses of their own. Even if your parents or in-laws are not the best examples, you can choose to break the cycle and create a positive example through your own life and marriage, which will also create a blessing for your children and their children.

Choose to focus on the positive. Your parents and your spouse's parents have likely done much more for you than you have realized. The prayers they have offered for you and the sacrifices they have made have blessed you in ways you can't calculate or adequately repay. So give your parents and in-laws honor and show them gratitude. Live with integrity, and you will make their hearts happy. Even if your parents or in-laws have not done much that is worthy of honor, as you follow God's command to honor them, you'll also be honoring your Father in heaven.

We have seen these two principles beautifully put into practice by our friend Elena. We met Elena several years ago and have come to see her as the epitome of grace. We can feel her love for the Lord whenever she walks in the room. In fact, this quality is what drew her husband, Oscar, to her decades ago. They were both young Christians when they met, and they progressed quickly toward marriage, though their families thought they were a bit too young. Throughout their decades-long marriage, Oscar's family, especially his father, Vic, always treated Elena poorly. When not ignoring her, he would speak to her unkindly. Vic was not very kind to Oscar or the grandchildren either. Over the years, this behavior caused Elena and Oscar to feel discouraged, angry, frustrated, and at times, doubtful that Vic would ever change. They set up some clear boundaries to protect their marriage and family (a topic we will discuss later), and they continued to reach out to Vic and show him respect. Oscar and Elena kept believing by faith that the Lord would one day heal their relationship with Vic.

God eventually answered their prayers but not in the way they expected. Shortly after Elena and Oscar retired, they were enjoying time with their children and grandkids. Then Oscar suddenly died. The entire family was devastated. At the funeral, Elena was not sure how Vic would respond or if either of them would really want to continue any sort of relationship. Vic had never made much effort to see his grandchildren or great-grandchildren in the past, so why would he want to start now? Elena figured that over time Vic would simply stop answering her calls, but what she did not know at the time was that the Lord had been softening his heart. The death of his son made Vic realize how he had squandered time with his loved ones. It was as though Vic could finally see what mattered most for the first time in his life.

After Oscar's funeral, Elena would call to check in with Vic, as she had done for many years, but something began to change whenever she called. His voice and demeanor were different. Vic seemed eager to talk to her and hear all about her life and what was happening with the kids and grandkids, and he even asked her to pray for him. Elena considered this transformation a true miracle. She felt as if Vic had become a different person, and at first, she was skeptical of the "new Vic." Elena waited for him to return to his old, disgruntled self. She had experienced so much heartache with the loss of her husband, and while she wanted to have a thriving relationship with her father-in-law, Elena was afraid of feeling her hopes dashed in the end. Even so, she continued to call and visit Vic and show him honor in the way she spoke to him and about him to other people. Elena continued to trust that the Lord was doing a miracle in her father-in-law's heart and in their family.

In our recent conversation with Elena, she teared up as she recounted how she has grown to love Vic as a second father over the past couple of years. She radiated with joy as she told us stories of how he requested she be one of the people by his side during a medical procedure. Elena talked about how Vic would check in with her to see how her day had gone. She counts it as a true miracle from the Lord for her father-in-law and for her. The Lord did a work in Elena's heart as well. Through her deep grief and heartache over the loss of her beloved husband, God surprised her with the support she received from her father-in-law. Even though Vic had caused pain and disappointment for her for many years, Elena and Oscar's willingness to show honor to him, along with God's amazing grace and mercy, made her restored relationship with her father-in-law possible. Elena and Vic's story serves as an important reminder for all of us to keep praying and believing that God is working things together for our good and His glory even in our most heartbreaking circumstances and even when we cannot see it. We can only ask that God would give us the grace to show kindness and honor to our parents and in-laws, even when they have not earned it.

Love what God loves and hate what He hates

Since God is the embodiment of love, some people are surprised to learn the Bible also says God is capable of "hate." We might scratch our heads in confusion and wonder how an all-loving God can hate anything, but He does. The Bible says it is precisely because God so fully loves His children that He's capable of fiercely hating those things that harm them or keep them from having an intimate relationship with Him.

Proverbs 6 is a window into the mind and heart of our loving heavenly Father. It also lists *seven things God hates*, each of which is an action that directly harms God's children and sabotages His blessings for them. Each thing injures the victims of the heinous actions and hurts the perpetrators who dehumanize themselves as they devalue God's laws and other people.

> There are six things the LORD hates—
>   no, seven things he detests:
> haughty eyes,
>   a lying tongue,
>   hands that kill the innocent,
> a heart that plots evil,
>   feet that race to do wrong,
> a false witness who pours out lies,
>   a person who sows discord in a family (Proverbs 6:16–19).

We should also think of the items on this list as the recipe for sabotaging unity in families. Jesus said, "Blessed *are* the peace-makers" (Matthew 5:9 NKJV), and everything on this list creates chaos instead of peace. We must safeguard our minds, hearts, and motives to keep from falling into these traps that can stir up division and drama in our families.

Consider each thing the writer of Proverbs lists:

1. God hates eyes that look down on other people because He has created every person in *His* image with dignity and eternal significance.

2. God hates a tongue that speaks lies because it is the truth that sets us free.

3. God hates hands that shed innocent blood because He never wants His children to suffer needless harm.

4. God hates a heart that harbors evil motives because such a heart makes no room for Jesus, our only Savior and Lord.

5. God hates feet that race toward sin because sin hurts everyone.

6. God hates a dishonest witness because false testimony per-
    verts the path of justice.

7. God hates someone who stirs up drama and division in a
    family because He wants His children to live together in love
    and unity.

God calls us to be people after His own heart. While we should
obviously stay away from the actions on this list in Proverbs 6, God
calls us to do more than that. In the list we find clarity about God's
plans and purposes for our lives. When we choose to continue
walking with God and learning from Him, then we direct our hearts
toward loving what He loves and hating what He hates.

> When we choose to continue walking
> with God and learning from Him, then we
> direct our hearts toward loving what He
> loves and hating what He hates.

Jesus expressed righteous anger, which caused Him to turn
over the money changers' tables in the Temple and drive them
out with a whip made from cords (see John 2:15–16). Jesus, who
was and is the embodiment of love, was capable of this holy rage
because He has the heart of God. Jesus' love for people caused
Him to become enraged at the behaviors He saw. The merchants
on the Temple grounds were exploiting people, and they were
occupying the only area in the Temple complex where the Jewish
religious leaders allowed Gentiles (non-Jews) to pray and worship the God of Israel.

Many people read the story of Jesus cleansing the Temple and
are puzzled by it. They think of it as a weak emotional moment in
an otherwise stellar ministry, but that is missing the point. Jesus did

not suddenly become angry at those who prevented the worship of God; rather, God has always opposed barriers that prevent access to Him. The apostle Matthew records Jesus' words:

> He said to them, "The Scriptures declare, 'My Temple will be called a house of prayer,' but you have turned it into a den of thieves!" (Matthew 21:13).

Jesus did not say, "I just got angry for a trivial reason." He said, "The Scriptures declare," and indeed they do. Look at these two passages of Scripture Jesus had in His mind when He said, "The Scriptures declare":

> I will also bless the foreigners who commit themselves to the LORD,
>   who serve him and love his name,
> who worship him and do not desecrate the Sabbath day of rest,
>   and who hold fast to my covenant.
> I will bring them to my holy mountain of Jerusalem
>   and will fill them with joy in my house of prayer.
> I will accept their burnt offerings and sacrifices,
>   because my Temple will be called a house of prayer for all
>   nations (Isaiah 56:6–7).

> Don't you yourselves admit that this Temple, which bears my name, has become a den of thieves? Surely I see all the evil going on there. I, the LORD, have spoken! (Jeremiah 7:11).

A random idea to stage a protest did not pop into Jesus' head in the Temple. God had been standing against those who prevented people from getting to know Him all along. Jesus knew His Father's heart was for all people to have access to Him, so the anger that spurred Jesus to turn over the merchant tables was the same emotion that caused Him to go to the cross. It is the same feeling God has forever had toward humanity. Jesus always opposes anything that keeps people from reaching God, even when it costs Him His life.

There are times when we should feel a righteous anger. There are occasions when we must allow that righteous anger to prompt us to act. When we see people being prevented from fully experiencing God's calling on their lives, it should upset us. When we see the vile exploitations of people because of human trafficking, we should fight for their freedom. When we see lies perverting the course of justice, we should boldly declare the truth and willingly fight to protect it. When we see people commit injustice, it should compel us to sacrifice our own comforts to protect those whom they injure.

One important caveat we should mention is that we are not qualified to judge every aspect of other people's lives. Only God can do that. If we are not careful, we might fall prey to legalism and completely miss Jesus' heart, like the Pharisees of Jesus' day who loved rules more than they loved God. If righteous anger stirs within you, then direct it first at your own sin. Only then will you have the humility necessary to remove the plank from your own eye before helping others take the speck of sawdust out of their eyes (see Matthew 7:3–5).

> God will not hold you accountable for how others treated you, but He will call on you to answer for how you treated them.

You will not always be able to control how your family or in-laws behave, but you will always have complete control of your *own* actions and responses. God will not hold you accountable for how others treated you, but He will call on you to answer for how you treated them. Show the same love and respect to others that you desire for yourself. Through your words and actions, you can be a light to your family even during dark and divisive moments. In time, God will honor your faith-filled actions.

Putting God's Word into practice

If you are an in-law parent, then please make it a joyful experience when someone marries one of your kids and enters your family. Be loving. Be accepting. Be encouraging. As a mother-in-law or father in-law, you have enormous power to set the tone from the very beginning of your relationship with your child's new family. You can either be a great blessing or a great burden to them. Your actions will either draw them in with love or repel them with criticism. The future of your family depends on what you choose.

Likewise, when you marry into a family, be respectful. Be loving. Be encouraging. Work hard to create unity even amid diversity. Celebrate your in-laws' traditions. Honor their legacy. Make it easy for your spouse to keep a healthy relationship with them. As far as it depends on you, live at peace with everyone and show honor to your spouse's family (see Romans 12:18).

In 1 Corinthians 13:4–7, the apostle Paul mentions 10 biblical traits that should guide our relationships. We have applied them to the in-law relationship.

1. Be patient with yourself, your spouse, your in-laws, and even God as you navigate making these relationships stronger and healthier.

2. Always speak and act kindly toward your in-laws and speak kindly about them to others.

3. Resist the urge to be jealous of your in-laws.

4. Be willing to listen to what your in-laws have to say and do not let pride keep you from doing so.

5. Show respect and honor to your in-laws by caring about their perspectives.

6. Be willing to compromise at times and do your best to pursue peace for all parties.

7. Assume the best of your in-laws but also be willing to address issues in a healthy way when they arise.

8. Fight against resentment by being honest with your spouse about any issues.

9. Protect your marriage and the peace in your home by collaborating with your spouse to create healthy boundaries with your extended family.

10. Keep praying for your marriage and family and hold onto the hope that God is the God of restoration and peace.

Even if your in-laws do not currently embody these traits, you do not need to wait for them to reciprocate your kindness. By your own actions, show the kinds of positive behaviors you hope to see from them.

In short, treat your in-laws the way you want to others to treat you, which is the Golden Rule Jesus taught (see Matthew 7:12). It should be our standard for all relationships, including the ones we have with our in-laws. When you honor them, you are also honoring God, honoring your spouse, and laying a solid foundation for future generations.

If you are already following these guidelines and not seeing these traits reciprocated, then keep praying for change. Keep pursuing healing. If necessary, put healthy boundaries and guidelines in place to protect your heart, your sanity, and your marriage. We will explore what those boundaries and guidelines should be in the next chapter.

It is often helpful to talk to a Christian counselor or to reach out to one of our amazing marriage mediators at www.xomarriage .com/help. You do not have to navigate this complicated road on your own. Help is available.

CHAPTER 1

Study Guide

for Individuals and Groups

Group leaders should prepare prior to the group meeting with the following steps:

- *Review the Introduction and Chapter 1.*

- *Read the book of Ruth; Proverbs 6:16–19, and 1 Corinthians 13:4–7.*

- *Choose one discussion question and one reflection question for group engagement in case time runs short.*

- *Pray for each group member by name. Ask the Lord to prepare their hearts and minds.*

- *If possible, silence your cell phone and remove any other distractions. Be fully present for your group and prepare to see lives transformed by God.*

Chapter 1 Summary

When you marry your spouse, you marry their family, but you will also meet new challenges. The Bible's example of Ruth and Naomi's relationship shows us that the in-law relationship can be a source of great blessing. God honored Ruth's devotion to Naomi and blessed her for it, and He blessed all the nations of the world through her lineage, which runs through King David and Jesus Christ.

God will honor us as we show respect for our parents and our spouse's parents. We should choose to focus on the good rather than the bad. We show our respect by living with honor and integrity ourselves and by forgiving our parents and in-laws. When we extend grace to them, we give a good example to the generations that come after us.

God wants us to love what He loves and hate what He hates. Jesus will always oppose anything that keeps people from reaching God. However, we are not qualified to judge every aspect of others' lives—only God can do that. If we are not careful, then we can fall prey to legalism. We cannot control how our families or in-laws behave, but we can always control our *own* actions and responses. God does not hold us accountable for how others treat us, but we will have to answer for the way we treat others. By our actions, we can show the kind of love and respect we want for ourselves. God will honor our faith-filled actions.

If you are an in-law parent, make it a joyful experience when someone enters your family by marriage. You can either be a great blessing or a great burden to them. The future of your family depends on what you choose. If you marry into a family, then be respectful, loving, and encouraging. Work hard to create unity even amid diversity. Do not wait for others to reciprocate your kindness. Live and behave in the way you would like to see others act. In any case, pray for change, pursue healing, and set healthy boundaries if necessary.

Discussion

1. What does it mean to you when you hear that when you marry, you also marry into the family?

2. When you look at the story of Ruth and Naomi, what part of that account gives you the most hope? What gives you the most questions?

3. As you read the list of behaviors Paul teaches from 1 Corinthians 13:4–7, which ones are the easiest for you to follow? Which ones are the most difficult?

Reflection

1. How should you respond when you see actions that are hurtful or cause division?

2. How should you respond when your in-laws do not treat you or your spouse with kindness?

3. When you evaluate your relationship with your in-laws, what are some of the actions you can take to improve your relationship with them?

4. How can you show more respect for your in-laws even when they do not show respect to your or your spouse?

Prayer

Father God, thank You for giving me the gift of my spouse. I believe that You are the Author of marriage, and You want me to live in harmony with my spouse and their parents or with my child's spouse. I know You are working through all circumstances for Your divine purposes. Show me how to respond when a spirit of division tries to take root in our family. When the enemy tries to distract us, please remind us to fix our eyes on You. Even when we experience conflict, help me to respond with love. Show me when I need to set up healthy boundaries. I believe that You are with me in every circumstance, and I trust You to work all things for my good. My hope is in You. In Jesus' name, Amen.

How to Leave & Cleave

Claire and Carlos were college sweethearts who could not wait to get married. They planned to marry soon after graduation. Since both Claire and Carlos were busy students finishing their coursework, Claire's mom eagerly stepped in to help coordinate the wedding. Claire and Carlos were glad to delegate some of the planning, and Claire's mom was happy to take the lead. She was a great event planner who had not been able to have a big wedding herself. In many ways, this was a dream come true for her to finally have an opportunity to plan her ideal wedding.

Both families expressed genuine enthusiasm about the upcoming wedding, and everything seemed blissfully perfect for the young couple as the big day approached. The wedding was all they hoped it would be, and it felt like a fairy tale as the new bride and groom rode in a horse-drawn carriage from the reception as friends and family cheered them on. They were so excited to finally start life together as husband and wife.

After a tropical honeymoon, the tanned couple met Claire's parents at the airport to go back to her parents' home and open the remaining wedding gifts and talk about the wedding and honeymoon. When they pulled into the driveway and everyone got out of the car, Carlos hugged Claire and whispered something into her ear. She smiled and said, "Okay. I will."

As Carlos and Claire's dad went into the house, Claire's mom grabbed her and asked sternly, "What did Carlos just whisper to you?" "Oh, it was nothing, Mom," Claire replied. Then with aggression that genuinely frightened Claire, her mom forcefully backed her up against the garage door. With a condescending and menacing tone, her mom said, "You listen to me, little girl. Just because you're married, don't think you can start keeping secrets from your mother!" Then she backed away and left. The encounter shook Claire, especially when her mother later acted as if nothing had happened. The new couple tried to enjoy opening their wedding gifts before leaving.

Claire's first post-wedding encounter with her mother had been deeply unsettling, and it set the tone for some dark days ahead. Carlos had always had the opinion that Claire had a bizarre and almost co-dependent relationship with her mom, but he was too focused on his relationship with Claire to give it much consideration. He knew Claire's mom could also be one of the most fun-loving and enjoyable people to be around when things were going well. The young couple naively dismissed many warning signs that had been present all along. They were busy with life and optimistic that any unhealthy family dynamics would simply "work themselves out" once they were married.

As newlyweds, Claire and Carlos quickly learned that things would certainly *not* work themselves out by ignoring them. Claire's mom seemed to be caught in an unhealthy vortex. They experienced her emotional outbursts, inconsistent standards, unrealistic demands, and a myriad of other erratic behaviors. The stress became unbearable for the young couple. Claire's dad was a kind, reasonable man, but he also seemed powerless to change the situation. He had spent most of his marriage as a peacemaker and an appeaser, and he had also unwittingly become an enabler for his wife's unhealthy behavior.

Claire was also a pleaser, both by nature and by her upbringing. She had always jumped through whatever hoops her mom demanded of her. As Claire was growing up, she learned to navigate her mom's moods, emotional outbursts, and unreasonable demands. Now, however, Claire was a married woman. Even so, she still could not seem to please her mom. Claire's mom appeared to be threatened by Claire's marriage. With a new husband in Claire's life, her mom's influence seemed to wane. As Claire brought her approval-seeking behaviors into her marriage, they were sabotaging her mental health and her relationship with her new husband.

The power struggle with Claire's mother continued for years. When tensions were at their worst, Claire reached out to her dad for support in navigating the tumultuous situation. She wanted help confronting her mom about the abusive behavior. Claire's dad sympathized, but he offered little help because of his own fear, exhaustion, or indifference. Her dad's lack of support felt every bit as disappointing as her mom's toxic behavior. Claire had always felt close to her parents, but for the first time in her life, she felt abandoned by both of them.

Claire and Carlos both wanted to salvage the relationships with her parents while also protecting their own marriage, but they didn't know where to start. Desperate for answers, they eventually scraped together enough money to meet with a marriage counselor. The counselor wisely helped the couple identify the gaslighting, unhealthy interactions, and unrealistic demands from Claire's mom and then helped them construct a practical plan to establish healthy boundaries.

Enforcing those boundaries would prove to be a messy business since no one had ever held Claire's mom accountable for her actions. Once her mom finally experienced boundaries for the first time, Claire experienced rage and unhinged outbursts from her mom.

Throughout the whole ordeal, Claire felt the constant tension between being a good daughter and being a good wife, which sometimes made her feel as though she was failing at both. She had subconsciously built much of her identity around being a good daughter, but as a wife she was out from under her parent's authority. Rather than receive their support, her mom bombarded her with the message that she was a terrible daughter who no longer cared for her family. Although her mom's reckless words were untrue, they still cut deep and triggered a great deal of anxiety.

Claire's world felt upside down. She had entered her marriage certain that the honeymoon phase would be blissful, but she never got to experience that newlywed bliss. Instead, she and Carlos experienced perpetual frustration and tension. Joy and romance marked their courtship, but it was quickly replaced with a heavy fog as they grieved the unnecessary loss of what should have been a special time.

The path forward was long and arduous, and while healing eventually came, it took a long time. It also took a lot of prayer, many hours of counseling, lots of boundaries, frequent messy conversations, and an enormous amount of patience and trust in God to work through it all. Moving away from their hometown also helped Claire and Carlos in the healing process.

The couple moved more for a job opportunity than to escape the situation, but once they landed in a new town, the very air they breathed felt like freedom. Before moving, they had never felt fully independent. A shift occurred that felt almost supernatural once they put down roots in the new place. Finally, Claire and Carlos felt as if they had their *own* family. At last, they experienced release from their parents' overarching authority. They felt peace and freedom in their new surroundings, solely under God's authority.

Every couple must learn to "leave and cleave."

The move helped Claire and Carlos see the whole situation from a brand-new perspective. It empowered them to interact with Claire's parents in a more productive way. While their decision to transfer to the new place was initially met with great resistance from Clair's mom, it caused her parents to soften their hearts and proved to be the turning point everyone needed to move forward in a healthy way.

Carlos and Claire later would say that their faith-filled decision to move away was the single most significant choice they ever made for the health of their marriage and family. God does not call everyone to move away from home, but every couple must learn to "leave and cleave," even if they choose to stay in their hometown.

What does it really mean to "leave and cleave"?

This explains why a man leaves his father and mother and is joined to his wife, and the two are united into one.

—Genesis 2:24

One of the Bible's most famous quotes about marriage comes near the very beginning. Genesis 2:24 varies by translation, but the message is identical. It is the most succinct and powerful blueprint for marriage ever recorded. This text gives a clear picture of God's vision for marriage, which requires *three distinct steps:*

1. Leave the family of origin.

God does not expect us to abandon our families, cut all ties with them, or lose our individual personalities. However, we must break from our parents' authority, structure, and often the physical location from the time we were single to make room for our own new family. The word "cleave" comes the Hebrew word *baqa*, which means 'to cleave, break open or through.'[1] Although we each have been rooted in our original families, when we join our spouse in holy matrimony, we consciously choose to break off from our original roots and replant a combined root in new soil with our new spouse. We stay rooted in God. It is a beautiful new planting, but it can also be a major adjustment because we are uprooting ourselves and entering a new environment—a new garden where we can learn how to thrive together with a new partner with God's help. Ideally, our family and community will support this new life with a new spouse. However, when our family of origin doesn't understand this concept or feels threatened by the process, it can feel like part of our root system has been left behind. It is then that we feel pulled at by both sides until our roots begin to fray, get thinner and thinner, and eventually snap. For various reasons, many individuals are never able to fully complete this first step in the three-step process. As a result, they never experience the deep intimacy marriage was designed to have.

2. Join and unite together.

Are you familiar with the phrase "leave and cleave"? The original Hebrew word for this action is *dabaq*. It is related but carries a different meaning than *baqa*. *Dabaq* describes the process of cling-ing together. It means 'to catch by pursuit: abide fast, cleave (fast together), follow close (hard after), to be joined (together), keep (fast).'[2] We imagine this like our two root systems being planted together, intertwining and growing stronger to the point of being nearly impossible to separate. This process requires nakedness—physically, mentally, and emotionally. Having sex is an important part of this joining process, but cleaving consists of more than simply making love. It is letting go of everything else in your life so you can hold each other completely. This process requires faith and complete commitment. It is the deliberate act of letting go of every other earthly bond so you will be able to embrace your spouse completely and wholeheartedly with a level of intimacy and commitment above all other people or things.

3. Embrace complete commitment and nakedness.

God Himself supernaturally completes this last step. He makes two individuals into "one flesh." God creates a spiritual unity, which mingles our very souls together. We still, of course, keep our indi-vidual identities, but now and for the rest of our lives, we're tied together with a bond of love only God could have orchestrated.

That is marriage. That is real intimacy. It is what God intends for you and your spouse.

Why do so many couples never experience that kind of supernatural intimacy? It is because they have not completed the first or second step of the process. The steps must take place in the proper order. God is a God of order, and He is not going to jump to the third step before you've done the necessary work on the first two. You have to leave, and you have to cleave. Until you do, you are essentially swimming upstream with one arm tied behind your back. You're not in full partnership with your spouse, and you're opening yourself up to all sorts of confusion and drama with your family and your in-laws.

When a spouse puts parents ahead of the marriage

Lately, I (Ashley) have talked with several wives who feel like they have hit a wall in their marriages. All of these women will tell you that they have a happy, thriving marriage in almost every way except for one huge elephant in the room—the relationship their husband has with his mother. As a quick disclaimer, this is a not a gender-specific issue. Unhealthy parent-child relationships can undoubtedly happen on both sides of the wedding aisle. However, I want to address the mother-son relationship specifically because I encounter it most often and have received so many messages related to it over the years. And even if you do not feel like this is an issue in your in-law relationships, the lessons from this apply to other in-law dynamics as well.

Let's unpack this relationship a bit more. Wives dealing with this dynamic feel pushed aside whenever their mother-in-law is around because their husband will place his mother's needs, desires, and opinions ahead of his wife's. These mothers-in-law will criticize how the wife keeps the house, dresses, disciplines the kids, and tends to their husband's needs. These wives really want good relationships with their mothers-in-law, but they don't feel accepted by them. Instead of healthy, supportive relationships, they have negative, conflicting relationships in which both women feel threatened by each other.

One wife wrote to me stating that her husband would talk to his mother on the phone approximately eight times per day but would often not answer the wife's call. If he did answer, he gave his wife the impression he did not feel like talking to her. This wife also said that during these calls to his mother, her husband was willing to share more details about his hopes, fears, and dreams than he was willing to share with her. This pattern hurt her deeply because it seemed as though her husband did not trust her enough to share those parts of himself with her. When she asked him about it, he was dismissive of her concerns.

As I read this wife's story, my heart felt a great burden. I could sense her frustration, hurt, anger, and confusion. She married her husband, but she felt as though her husband had really wed his own mother! This wife knew that something had to change, so she and her husband sought out a Christian counselor who helped them start the challenging work of establishing boundaries with the husband's mother. However, as with most co-dependent relationships, it took a long time for her husband to see how unhealthy things really were in his relationship with his mother. He did not realize he was actually preventing himself from having a healthy, connected relationship with his wife.

Whenever I speak with women whose husbands prioritize their relationship with their mothers over their wives, I notice that these wives share several common emotions. They feel disrespected, patronized, and overshadowed by their mothers-in-law. More than anything else, they are frustrated with their husbands for not standing up for them and for allowing this behavior to continue.

As a married couple, we should do whatever we can to love, respect, and keep peace with our extended families, but it must never be at the expense of our marriages. Our parents must understand that it is not their place to govern their married children

or their children's marriages. We need their support and encouragement, and we welcome their wisdom when we ask for it. But
they still need to respect us, our spouse, our marriage, and our
privacy. So how do we respond when they don't? Do we simply
allow them to continue undermining our spouses and marriages
without objection? Certainly not.

A wife should never feel as if she must compete with her husband's mother for his love, respect, and adoration. As a husband,
you may be having these very conversations with your wife right
now, and you are probably thinking, *My mom is a grown woman
who makes her own decisions. I cannot help how she feels about my
wife or how she chooses to treat her.* This is a huge issue, and you
must address it right away. Your mom needs to hear *you* tell her
that her controlling, passive-aggressive, or polarizing demeanor
towards your wife and marriage must stop. You must tell your
mother that she will have to speak kindly about your wife in your
presence, or the conversation will end. Make sure you speak to your
mother in the most respectful way possible, but you must address
the situation directly. The health of your marriage depends on it.

> A wife should never feel as if she must
> compete with her husband's mother for
> his love, respect, and adoration.

I know these conversations are uncomfortable. Emotions will
run high because you will be addressing difficult issues with those
you love and respect. That is the reason why these conversations
must happen before matters grow worse. I have seen unhealthy
extended-family dynamics play a huge role in decisions for couples
to separate or divorce. There is too much at stake!

You can have both a great marriage and a great relationship
with your mom, but your marriage must come first. Besides, the
kind of love you feel for your wife should be categorically different

from the kind of love you feel for your mother. You can love them both, but you must care for your wife's needs before you tend to your mother's. A time may come when you will need to care for an aging or ill parent, but you can still prioritize your marriage first while meeting your parents' needs.

When we marry, our relationship with our parents must change. Our first allegiance belongs to God, then our spouse, then our children (if we have them), and then our parents. This order is not something we created; rather, it's how God designed marriage and family. As we discussed earlier in this chapter, Genesis 2:24 says, "That is why a man leaves his father and mother and is united to his wife, and they become one flesh" (NIV). Unity is necessary in marriage.

Two cannot become one unless they are unified, which means a husband and a wife must be on the same page and moving in the same direction physically, emotionally, and spiritually. Unity cannot happen if a husband feels like loving his wife will somehow keep him from loving and respecting his mother. Loving your mother and loving your wife are two completely different experiences.

Husbands, your mother will always be a part of you. She raised you and was the first woman to love you. She will love you forever, but she is *not* your wife. Your mom may have a hard time letting go, but she must relinquish control for the sake of your marriage. Your mom will always be your mother, and you will always be her son. Nothing will change that. But your wife deserves your full devotion. You vowed to love her, protect her, serve her, and even give your very life for her. That's a very different kind of love, one that can only be experienced when you offer your full heart to your spouse.

Whether it's excessive and misplaced devotion to our extended family relationships, spending too much time at the office, or not giving enough time to our families, we must talk about these issues with our spouses. Tell your spouse how much you love their devotion to family, how you respect their excellent work ethic, and how you admire their generosity. Then, gently but firmly remind them that all of life must be kept in balance. God never calls or equips us to do something detrimental to our marriage, which is our first loyalty and our primary ministry.

Complete Commitment

In His infinite wisdom, God knew we would need as much help as possible to navigate relationship dynamics in our families. For that reason, He has given us powerful examples throughout the Bible. We can know how marriage should be when it is done right. God's Word also issues some sobering warnings for what marriage can look like if we disregard God's guidelines. Some of the most powerful and practical examples for marriage in the Bible come directly through the example of Jesus Christ.

Many people share the common misconception that since Jesus lived His earthly life as a bachelor, we can't learn any marriage principles from Him. The truth is that Jesus spent His entire earthly life engaged to be married to us. The Bible says Jesus is the Bridegroom, and we (His Church) are the bride. In fact, the apostle Paul says Jesus' love for the Church has been in place even before the world was created (see Ephesians 1:4). Revelation chapter 19 tells us that we will celebrate a great wedding feast, sealing our eternal union with Jesus. This feast will last seven years, but the marriage celebration will last forever. Repeatedly, the Bible points to the marriage between God and His people.

Jesus, knowing He is our Bridegroom and the only perfect example of what a husband should be, shows us repeatedly what character traits are necessary for a healthy marriage. He shows us what it means to "leave and cleave" as He calls all of us to leave everything that's holding us back from being completely united with and committed to Him. Jesus says, "Whoever wants to be my disciple must deny themselves and take up their cross and follow me. For whoever wants to save their life will lose it, but whoever loses their life for me will find it" (Matthew 16:24–25 NIV). He gives Himself completely to us and expects our complete loyalty in return.

Jesus raises a high bar for our commitment to Him. He is not vague with His words. In fact, Jesus' blunt language scares away many would-be followers who aren't ready for the commitment He requires. Jesus says things such as, "If you love your father or mother more than you love me, you are not worthy of being mine; or if you love your son or daughter more than me, you are not worthy of being mine" (Matthew 10:37). This verse is sobering. Jesus tells us that He must be our *first* devotion. He describes a life of faith committed to Him, but since Jesus is our Groom and we are to be His bride, He also reveals an important truth about the commitment required for marriage. We must put our spouse before our parents and even before our children. Jesus' hierarchy for commitment is established by God from the beginning of Creation, and to ignore it is to invite chaos into our lives and homes.

We must put our spouse before our parents and even before our children.

The more you love Jesus, the more capacity you will have to love your spouse. The more you love your spouse, the more capacity you will have to love your children and your extended family. If we get God's hierarchy out of order, then love will diminish instead of grow. If we love our parents more than our spouse, then we won't fully love our spouse (or even our parents for that matter). Putting our children at the top of the list will create codependency instead of healthy love. It will also sabotage marriage. One of the best things you can do for your marriage is to love God with your whole heart. One of the best things you can do for your kids is to love your spouse and put them first. One of the best things you can do for your mental health and for the health of every relationship in your life is to respect the relational hierarchy God has established.

CHAPTER 2

Study Guide

for Individuals and Groups

Group leaders should prepare prior to the group meeting with the following steps:

- *Review Chapter 2.*
- *Read Genesis 2:24; Matthew 10:37; 16:24; and Ephesians 1:4.*
- *Choose one discussion question and one reflection question for group engagement in case time runs short.*
- *Pray for each group member by name. Ask the Lord to prepare their hearts and minds.*
- *If possible, silence your cell phone and remove any other distractions. Be fully present for your group and prepare to see lives transformed by God.*

Chapter 2 Summary

Genesis 2:24 says, "This explains why a man leaves his father and mother and is joined to his wife, and the two are united into one." This text gives a clear picture of God's vision for marriage, which requires *three distinct steps:*

1. Leave the family of origin.

2. Join and unite together.

3. Embrace complete commitment and complete nakedness.

Many wives say they are happy in their marriages except for their husband's relationship with his mother. A wife dealing with this dynamic feels pushed aside because her husband will place his mother's needs, desires, and opinions ahead of his wife's. In turn, the mother-in-law will criticize the wife and her actions. The wife feels disrespected, patronized, and overshadowed by her mother-in-law, as well as frustrated with her husband for not standing up for their relationship and allowing this behavior to continue.

As a married couple, we should do whatever we can to love, respect, and maintain peace with our extended families, but it must never be at the expense of our marriage. Parents must understand it is not their place to govern their grown children's lives or marriages. A wife should not feel as if she must compete with her husband's mother. The health of your marriage depends on it.

When we marry, our relationships with our parents must change. As we join with our new spouses, our first allegiance belongs to God, then our spouses, then our children (if we have them), and then our parents. It is how God designed marriage and family.

Jesus, our Bridegroom and the only perfect example of what a husband should be, shows us in Scripture what character traits are necessary for a healthy marriage. He shows us what it means to "leave and cleave" as He calls all of us to leave everything that's holding us back from being completely united with and committed to Him. Since Jesus is our Groom and we are to be His bride, He also reveals an important truth about the commitment required for marriage: we must put our spouse before our parents and even before our children. Jesus' hierarchy for commitment is established by God from the beginning of Creation, and to ignore it is to invite chaos into our lives and homes.

Discussion

1. How would you explain the concept of "leave and cleave" to a couple having conflict in this area?

2. What problems do you see in our society as a result of people's refusal to follow God's hierarchy of relationships (God first, spouse second, children third, parents fourth, and everyone else last)?

3. If you had a friend who felt as if they were in second place compared to their spouse's parents, what would you say to help them navigate the situation?

Reflection

1. God says we should not have anything *before* Him, but He also says we should not have anything *beside* Him (see Exodus 20:3). Most people would never admit to having something before God, but many have things that compete beside God. What do you need to confront in your life that threatens to compete with God?

2. In God's hierarchy, God is first, and our spouse is second. Is there anything or anyone in your life that is competing with your spouse? What or who is it?

3. What positive steps can you take right now to restore God's hierarchy in your life?

4. How can you let your spouse know that they are first in your life next to God?

Prayer

Father God, I ask You to forgive me for putting anything in front of You or competing alongside You. I know it is wrong, and I want to change my heart and mind. Help me as I take the necessary steps to put You on the throne of my life. As I make You my priority, help me to make my spouse second only to You. I need Your help and strength to restore and reprioritize anything I have gotten out of order. Thank You for the gift of my spouse. I never want to take them for granted. Use your Holy Spirit to convict me so that I will not get things out of order again. Thank you for caring about my life and how I live it with my spouse. In Jesus' name, Amen.

CHAPTER 3

10 Unhealthy Types of In-Laws

In our experience of working with thousands of couples, we have discovered 10 types of dysfunctional in-law relationships.[1] Now, we know there may be more types, and we also realize that some people can fit more than one type. However, most people tend to lean toward one of these as a dominant type. Each of these types carries unique dysfunctional traits and challenges.

Just as a doctor diagnoses an illness before selecting an appropriate treatment regimen, it's often necessary to diagnose the source of dysfunction in a relationship with in-laws before we can put a strategy in place. It's important to note that dysfunction influences an entire family system, and it's possible that you and your spouse both play key roles in the continuing problem. We all have issues and things we need to address!

In your life and marriage, you must remain vigilant and self-aware so you won't also fall into an unhealthy type of in-law. Be aware of your own relationship dynamics. Ask yourself if you are doing anything to perpetuate the dysfunction, even if inadvertently, instead of promoting healing. We will address some of those personal issues later, but for now we're going to focus on identifying the negative types of in-law relationships.

1. The Bullies

At any stage of life, dealing with a bully is demoralizing and exhausting. Many unhealthy relationships follow this dynamic, but in a marriage, there is a unique form of despair when your own parents or in-laws are engaged in the bullying.

Bullying in-laws use their power, whether real or perceived, to belittle, manipulate, criticize, intimidate, and control others. People are complex, so it's possible for a bully to have moments of genuine care and concern, but they always revert back to domineering and manipulative tactics, which make even the peaceful moments seem unsafe. You never know when the other shoe is about to drop.

When only one in-law is outwardly a bully, the silent or passive in-law tries to appease their spouse, which amounts to tacit approval for the bullying behavior. In this way, both in-laws are complicit and, therefore, equally accountable. Regardless of whether the passive in-law's silence stems from fear, indifference, or something else, their unwillingness to intervene on your behalf makes them culpable. We say this with one important qualifier: sometimes one in-law is caught in a long-term cycle of abuse, which may make it impossible to address the problem without serious repercussions. Perhaps more so than any other type on this list, bully in-laws must be given clear boundaries because without boundaries, they will inflict unmendable damage upon your marriage and family.

2. The Judges

In this dynamic, the in-laws act as judge (and jury) over every part of the extended family. Driven by the need to maintain control, they make the rules and set the standards. Judges often have some knowledge of the Bible, and they will use it to bolster their critiques by appealing to "biblical standards." However, their judgments are not necessarily motivated by a true desire to follow God's Word or help you and your spouse grow closer to Jesus. They cover their rationale with a veneer of faith-speak, but they act as legalistic Pharisees who issue non-Christlike judgments.

Some judges will not attempt to base their opinions on the Bible. They may not practice any faith, or they're not familiar enough with the Bible to wield and warp it for their own selfish purposes. In this case, they may have their own code of conduct, or they might make it up on the fly. Their customs and manners are inconsistent, and their judgments are based on their feelings rather than any real measure of healthy living or relationships. They will attempt to make you and your spouse play by their self-created rules, occasionally letting you know when you have succeeded but always informing you when you have failed.

If you are pleasers or peacemakers by nature (which both of us are), then navigating the rules and personalities of the judges in your life will be exceptionally difficult. This statement is true whether the judges in your life are in-laws, parents, other family members, friends, bosses, or co-workers. Our urges to make peace can lead us to defer to the dominant voices of the judges, but God calls us all to have courage. He expects us to look to Him as our only Judge. Otherwise, we will be giving other people the authority only God should have. If we put other humans in that place, then we aren't peacemakers—we are idol-makers. Remember, God is your authority, and the standard of conduct you follow is the Bible.

> God is your authority, and the standard of conduct you follow is the Bible.

One example of the judge dynamic occurs when an in-law visits the adult child's home and comments negatively on everything—furniture placement, temperature in the house, landscaping, and a host of other things related to the home. Judge in-laws might even take it upon themselves (without permission) to rearrange the furniture, adjust the temperature, or hire a landscaping company to overhaul the yard, while still expecting you to pick up the bill. In this instance, it's crucial for both spouses to communicate with each other because the one whose parent is acting as the judge may be so used to the behavior that they don't even realize it is happening. They don't see what their parent is doing as harmful and disrespectful. Once a couple recognizes the toxic behavior, it's important to address it in a loving way. This response to the parent might include saying, "That's one way to put the furniture, but we really like it this way," or "Hmm, that probably would look pretty, but we've worked really hard on the yard lately and love how it looks right now." If the judging in-law says something that is unmistakably hurtful, then the adult child of the judge should confront it by saying something like, "Ouch! That was harsh, Mom," or "Man, Dad, you are really taking the wind out of my sails." You can even say it with a hint of jest (and maybe a nervous laugh), but comments like these should get the point across to the judge that they have overstepped your home's boundaries and they need to back down. If they continue with hurtful comments, then you will need to plainly and calmly tell them that it is not okay to come into your home and talk to you and your spouse that way.

When anyone in your life, in-laws or otherwise, tries to step in and control your thoughts or behaviors to conform to their standards, you must lovingly and firmly reject those judgments. Do everything you can to show respect and promote harmony, but don't yield to unwarranted authority or judgment for the sake of peace, because that's not real peace.

3. The Elitists

Elitist in-laws feel as though they're really a big deal—*and you are not.* They will tend to look down on both you and others. Elitists might subtly or obviously let you know you're lucky to be associated with their family. They may even communicate that you will never truly be a part of their family. According to their warped value system, you will never measure up.

Pride is the enemy of intimacy. If your in-laws have wrapped themselves up in pride, then a healthy relationship is impossible. Elitist in-laws will miss out on experiencing the full life Christ has for them because they use superficial rather than eternal standards to value people and things. Their elitism puts a wedge in the family and causes you and your spouse to miss out on the intimacy you could have with them.

Even if you recognize their broken values, it still hurts to be rejected or dismissed by family members. Elitist behavior is especially hurtful when the disapproval is only aimed at the spouse who marries into the family. These in-laws might make statements that show their disapproval of you, pass judgment on your parents, or say things about your upbringing in an attempt to elevate themselves while putting down you and your family of origin.

If you find yourself facing the elitist dynamic, then you and your spouse must make the conscious choice not to accept that value system in your relationship. You do not have to play the same game by the same rules. Stand up for each other and remain united. Resist chasing after the approval of an elitist in-law. You do not need to gain their accolades so you can feel more worthy in their eyes. Yes, you should work to achieve all God has called you to do, but do it for His glory rather than the superficial approval of people who are operating from a shallow value system. Once you put your faith in Jesus Christ, believe you have been adopted by the King of kings. You are God's own child. He loves you completely and approves of you wholeheartedly. Once you fully embrace your identity and acceptance in Christ, you will realize that you do not need to chase after the approval of others.

We often see this in-law dynamic at play when one spouse comes from a family with wealth or advanced education while the other spouse's family does not. Sometimes, the family with more money or higher academic degrees assumes that the spouse raised without these things might lack a strong work ethic or even intelligence, so they approach the spouse from an elitist position and act as though the spouse is beneath their family. In this situation, both spouses must recognize what is really happening, and the spouse whose parents are acting in elitist ways must privately and lovingly draw their parents' attention to this behavior.

Now, we should always assume the best about our parents and give them the benefit of the doubt. They may not realize they are coming off this way. However, if the parents continue to act as elitists, as though they are (or their adult child is) too good for the spouse, then their adult child should calmly challenge their perspective. If you are the adult child, then remind your parents that you love your spouse and chose to marry them. Tell your parents that you want to have a good relationship with them, but you must first respect your partner. You cannot allow them to treat your spouse as someone beneath them. Remind your parents that everyone is part of a single family now with commonalities and differences, and your love for one another should not depend on things like money, education, pedigree, or upbringing. As always, pray with your spouse before these hard conversations, and ask the Lord to soften every heart. Trust God to give you the words that will resonate well with your parents and in-laws.

> Your love for one another should not depend on things like money, education, pedigree, or upbringing.

We want to leave one word of caution as you confront the elitist dynamic: make sure *you* don't give into *reverse elitism,* which is the temptation to create your own alternate value system in an effort to spite or compete with your parents or in-laws. Watch for the

urge to pass judgment on them for not measuring up to your standards. Set aside pride and the impulse to put them in their place
and choose to love them instead. You can be concerned when they
are blinded by the world's broken systems but continue to pray for
them. Sincere prayer will keep your heart in the right place.

4. The Takers

Humans are selfish by nature, but some people are more selfish
than others. If your in-laws are takers, then they will always try
to take whatever they can get. If you have financial means, then
they'll want your generosity at every turn. If you don't have a lot of
money, then they'll push for other things. For example, they may
want full access to your time or your children.

The taker in-law dynamic shows up in a lot of different scenarios. Parents or in-laws who demand time with your kids can
create a complicated situation. Obviously, active grandparents
can be a huge blessing. If they help create a healthy, unified, and
multi-generational family, then their presence in your children's
lives is almost always a great thing. But what if it is not healthy?
Some grandparents involve themselves with their grandchildren
in controlling ways, such as dominating the family's schedule or
trying to become greater authorities than the parents. They may
want to raise your kids in a different way and may even try to
undermine your standards because they feel like they know what
is best for their grandchildren.

Takers may also encourage your kids to keep secrets from you,
or they may not fully disclose things that happen to your kids while
they are under the grandparents' care. These behaviors are huge
breaches of trust and must be addressed head on in a kind and calm
way. You must remind your parents or in-laws that you love them
and are happy they want to spend time with your kids. You want to
encourage a strong grandchild-grandparent relationship. However,

they must respect your authority over your own children. If they continue to demand time and disregard your wishes as parents, then you must put some boundaries in place. For example, you may choose not to allow your kids to visit the grandparents unless you and your spouse are also present. We will address this issue in more detail later in the book.

Like most of the other dysfunctional relationships we discuss in this chapter, the taker is motivated by an unhealthy desire for control. Takers want to control you by possessing your resources, time, kids, or other areas of your life. If they expect you to give at a level that compromises your mental health, legitimate authority, or influence in your children's lives, then you have a moral obligation to stop the behavior. And, as in all cases, you must maintain unity in your marriage.

5. The Scorekeepers

Scorekeepers always keep a tally. You will always feel as though you are losing on their scorecard even if you don't know the game that is being played. Now, scorekeeping can take on different forms. In some situations, scorekeepers measure how much time you are spending with them versus other people and places. In other circumstances, scorekeepers will do a favor for you or give you a gift, but strings are attached. These are not really favors or gifts, and the scorekeeper will remind you of their generosity whenever they want something in return.

Similar to judges, scorekeepers unilaterally make their own rules and expect you to play by them. The rules are often inconsistent, and you will never be able to "win" because someone has rigged the game. The only authentic way to succeed is to stop playing the game.

One common scorekeeper game is to compare how much time you spend with the other set of in-laws. They will often voice their dissatisfaction, even if you are really trying to make things as fair as possible. You could keep a spreadsheet, and they would still question the data. You may feel as though you are a hamster caught in a never-ending wheel. You and your spouse must remember that if you are genuinely trying your best to be fair and kind everyone, then that is the best you can do. Exit the wheel. You cannot control the satisfaction of your in-laws, especially when they view themselves as victims or feel as though they are always doing or giving more than anyone else.

Keep reassuring your in-laws of your love. Tell them you are trying your best to have good relationships with both sides of the family. Then, if they continue to complain, respond by saying something such as, "I'm sorry you are disappointed, but we really are doing the best we can."

As with all these in-law dynamics, keep doing everything in your power to show respect. In some cases, you may even choose to yield to some of their preferences when they do not violate your own convictions. You and your spouse may agree to turn down some gifts or offers of "help" from scorekeepers. If the in-law pushes the issue and asks why you are making this choice, then you can tell them it's because you feel every gift seems to come with strings and expectations attached. Although you appreciate their generosity, you'd rather not put yourself in a position to owe anything to anyone.

6. The Gaslighters

We think this may be the most difficult in-law dynamic on the list. In fact, dealing with a gaslighter in any area of your life can lead to frustration and despair. Gaslighting has become a popular term in today's culture, with different people using it in different ways. When we say *gaslighting*, we are referring to "a patterned, repetitive set of manipulation tactics that makes someone question reality."[2] Gaslighters constantly rewrite history and redefine reality to give themselves the upper hand in relationships. They try to make anyone who disagrees with them question their own judgment. In the worst cases, gaslighters' targets start to feel as though they are crazy. Gaslighters rarely apologize unless their remorse is part of a broader scheme to control others by means of emotional manipulation. However, they do expect constant apologies from others.

Given the intensity of gaslighting, it may surprise you to find out that some gaslighters are actually unaware of what they're doing.[3] According to *Psychology Today*, "Even if a person is practicing gaslighting without being consciously aware of it, they may get a 'payoff' when their victim becomes more dependent on them."[4] It's a sick, twisted game of control. A person with narcissistic or sociopathic tendencies is especially dangerous, and in those cases, the only thing to do is remove yourself from the relationship.

Adult spouses who encounter gaslighter in-laws often witness tantrums and tears when they try to stand their ground or refuse to behave exactly as their in-law desires. It's possible for a gaslighter to cry, yell, stonewall, show affection, and stomp off in anger all in the span of one conversation. Manipulation becomes rampant in the relationship. Therefore, it is extremely important for a married couple to be on the same page as they face gaslighter antics. If a gaslighter parent raised you, then these kinds of shenanigans can feel normal. You may even find yourself making excuses for them. You might catch yourself thinking, *They mean well, but they are just high strung,* or *They are just passionate and love us so much that they get worked up sometimes.* If you find yourself inwardly or outwardly making excuses for gaslighting behavior, then by all means, please stop.

When you try to stand up to a gaslighting parent or in-law, a reasonable conversation can quickly escalate into a fight. The gaslighter counts on you standing down and giving in to whatever they want. At times, you may convince yourself it is easier that way, but you are really feeding their inner monster and doing harm to your relationships and your own mental health.

You may need to enlist a professional Christian counselor to help you begin setting boundaries with a gaslighter. After you have decided on these boundaries, you must firmly and kindly stick to them. Remember, boundaries are for the health of your marriage *and* your relationship with your parents or in-laws. You can't know or control how a gaslighter will react, but you can control your own actions and responses. If a gaslighter throws a tantrum, which is very common, then tell them you love them and are willing to have a conversation with them but only when they calm down and can really listen to what you have to say. Changing the way you communicate may require a professional mediator or counselor if they continue to disregard your boundaries and respond with manipulation.

> You can't know or control how a gaslighter will react, but you can control your own actions and responses.

If your in-laws are the gaslighting type, whether purposefully or subconsciously, start with the assumption that they don't fully realize the harm they're causing. Many gaslighters are unaware that their behaviors are malicious and unhealthy because they are working from a broken worldview. They may have felt powerless at some point in their past, so to survive, they think they need to control others as a means of self-preservation. Still, whether their motives are innocent or devious, the actions of a gaslighter can be very damaging, and it's important to bring the behavior to light and require a change.

7. The Separators

Separators constantly want to divide you and your spouse. They might regularly create family gatherings or vacations and invite only *their* family. While they try to preserve their family unit as they once knew it, their goal isn't to help your marriage thrive. Their actions show that they want to put a wedge between you and your spouse so that they can keep control over their "child" without your interference. They claim to be the ones who know what's "best" for their adult child, and their opinion always seems to count more than yours or your spouse's,

Separators are often unaware of the effects of their behavior. They may not operate out of malicious intent, but the results are still harmful. They will start from the position of "just wanting time" with their adult children. They may even work under the guise of protecting their kids, but the situation can quickly morph into unhealthy control, which excludes you from the family and even your own marriage. It is normal and healthy for parents to want one-on-one time with their adult children, but separators take this desire too far by only wanting their adult child at your expense. They might be polite to you, but they will make sure you know, subtly or directly, that you're never going to be part of *their* family.

The first step to take when you realize separators are at work is to make your spouse aware. Show them this chapter. In many cases, it's happening simply because the family is trying to maintain the flow and rhythm they had before you entered the picture. They may be unaware that they're consistently excluding you. They might have assumed you didn't want to participate in certain activities without realizing they exclude you even when you are present. As with all the unhealthy dynamics in this chapter, you must communicate with your spouse and decide together what health should look like in your marriage. As you approach this situation, be sure to do your part to foster your unified healthy vision. Your new approach may require you to insist your spouse come on family vacations, even when your parents try to arrange it to be just "our family." If your parents don't like this new direction and give you a hard time about it, then you must consistently remind them that you are a married person now, and you want to include your spouse in family activities. You may need to appeal to their hearts by helping them see that when they don't include your spouse, it hurts your heart and your spouse's heart as well.

8. The Smotherers

Dealing with smotherers can be a tricky situation because they are usually operating out of sweet and selfless motives. But when your in-laws want to help and be involved *too much,* then you can end up feeling smothered. If one or both of your in-laws is a helper by nature, then they may go overboard by wanting to be at your house constantly and trying to assist with projects (sometimes even projects you hadn't planned on doing). They might bring meals over all the time. They may want to watch the grandbabies so much that they're seeing your kids more than you do.

Addressing this dynamic is delicate. It's important to show gratitude for your in-laws' kindness, but it's also important to establish some healthy boundaries. Many smotherers have looked forward for many years to welcoming new in-laws who will marry their children and give them grandbabies. Once this special time finally arrives, they just can't help themselves because of their enthusiasm. They're feel as though they are living out their very specific vision for how things should be. They have dreamt about how an ideal multigenerational family should work. In some cases, they may be overcompensating for the feelings they have toward in-laws or parents who didn't help them in their early years, so they're committed to being different. As they overcorrect, they can also overstep reasonable boundaries.

You and your spouse must communicate about how often and how much you would like to see your parents or in-laws, especially when it comes to them visiting your home. Your home is your domain, so you and your spouse must decide who visits and how long they stay. If your parents or in-laws are visiting a little too often and staying a little too long to the point where you feel like you and your spouse don't have time and space to tend to your marital relationship, then you need to set some parameters. In this scenario, the spouse whose parents overstay their welcome should sit down with them and explain that you are trying to cultivate a strong marriage, peaceful home, and unified family. Therefore, you would appreciate it if they could call and check with you before popping in for a visit. You might even consider creating a schedule where your parents or in-laws can come over for dinner once a week. This compromise will allow you and your spouse to prepare your minds and hearts so you can look forward to this time with them, rather than feeling bombarded by them. If they don't like these boundaries and only see them as limitations, then try to reassure them by reminding them how much you love and appreciate them but that you are also married adults who are building a life together. This conversation can be a little more complicated when grandkids are involved, which we will address in more detail later.

Your home is your domain, so you and your spouse must decide who visits and how long they stay.

9. The Chemically Imbalanced

When a family member or in-law isn't fully in their right mind, it can put you in a precarious position. Chemical imbalances may stem from chemical addiction to drugs or alcohol, which might require a family intervention. An imbalance might also come from other physical issues, such as hormone deficiencies for which the person needs medication. Encouraging necessary medications can be a delicate conversation and also might eventually require some sort of intervention.

If you have a parent or in-law who is chemically imbalanced, then encourage them to get help. Offer your support and encouragement but not your judgment. Let them know you want to be part of their life, but their current behaviors are preventing the possibility of a healthy relationship. Getting help for an addiction or getting medication for an imbalance could be the bridge to better health for them and make healthier relationships possible for the entire family. These types of interventions are usually most effective when led by the person's spouse and their own children, with in-laws and other relatives or friends providing support.

If a chemically imbalanced person refuses to get help, then you might have to put some firm boundaries in place. As always, make sure your boundaries are clear. Protect your own marriage and mental health, but establish these boundaries with the ultimate goal of reconciliation when you can observe healthier behaviors. In the meantime, even if it's from a distance, pray and do whatever you can to communicate your love and support until your chemically imbalanced loved one finally decides to get the help they need.

10. The Ghosts

The situation with a ghost can be heartbreaking. We are describing what happens when parents or in-laws intentionally vanish from your life. There can be a variety of reasons for this behavior. Perhaps one parent dies, and the other remarries. The new spouse might pull them in a different direction that doesn't seem to include you or your family anymore. Over time, contact becomes less and less frequent until you're not part of each other's lives at all anymore.

This dynamic is particularly heartbreaking when your own children start noticing that their grandparents don't seem to have any interest in their lives. They might feel personally rejected, which will mean you must delicately address the issue with your kids and make sure they realize none of this situation is their fault. It can be difficult to know what to say, but reassuring them of your own love for them is a good place to start. Also, remind them of God's unending love for them. It can go a long way in guarding their hearts through the disappointment of absentee grandparents.

There are countless factors that can lead family members to act as ghosts. As with the other unhealthy in-law dynamics we've discussed in this chapter, pray for restoration, do *your* part to rebuild the relationship, and give yourself permission to grieve losses. Try not to focus on their absence during special moments, such as holidays and milestones, but also don't act like these absentee family members don't exist. Still have pictures of them around the house. Continue looking at the photo albums and reminisce about the good times. If you feel sadness creeping in, then it's okay to take a break to grieve. We must walk through these emotions and not push them away. It's okay to be sad, but also pray and ask God to keep your heart soft and hopeful. He is with us and hears our prayers. He is our source of strength, especially when our hearts are broken. He sees our pain and knows how to put the pieces back together—even if our parents, in-laws, or other loved ones continue to act like ghosts in our lives.

Should our parents or in-laws eventually start coming back around, it may feel very awkward or even hurtful. It can seem as though we've been duped or as if we are just waiting for the other shoe to drop before they disappear once again. This experience can be maddening and potentially cause a lot of marital conflict. However, we should not let our anger, frustration, or disappointment bring out the worst in us. One of the healthiest steps we can take is to reach out to a professional Christian counselor so we can receive personal guidance and support. It might also be helpful to invite your parents or in-laws to come to Christian mediation with you. Now, they may scoff at this proposal, but if they do, explain that you love them and want to make sure all parties can be heard and understood. A Christian mediator is trained to help families achieve this give-and-take in a safe environment. The goal is help rebuild the relationship while also establishing healthy boundaries so unhealthy dynamics are not perpetuated. We will discuss more of the nuts and bolts for dealing with ghost in-laws, as well as the issue of estrangement, later in the book.

———————

In the next chapter, we will explore how to set up effective boundaries in real-life in-law situations. We'll also look at how and when to pursue reconciliation when relationships are damaged or even severed. In addition, we will discuss the need for personal humility and self-awareness throughout the entire process. Everyone should avoid retaliation and the temptation to take on the same negative relationship dynamics they have experienced from others as a means to combat unhealthy behaviors. For instance, don't become a judge who complains about an in-law who judges. Don't become a scorekeeper by holding on to every infraction as ammunition you can use in the future. Don't become a ghost who simply disappears at the first sign of difficulty. It's natural to want to retaliate and fight fire with fire, but you don't have to follow that nature. Even if someone has been hurtful to you, Jesus calls us to a higher and better standard that is far superior to retaliation and revenge.

As a final disclaimer, we recognize there might be times when cutting off all contact (whether temporarily or permanently) is the only healthy solution to protect your own family. We will discuss those kinds of situations in the coming chapters. It may be necessary as a last resort, but it should never be our first instinct. God's plan is always reconciliation and unity whenever possible. We're called to do our part to live at peace with those in our lives. The apostle Paul wrote, "Never pay back evil with more evil. Do things in such a way that everyone can see you are honorable. Do all that you can to live in peace with everyone" (Romans 12:17–18). But when other people consistently refuse to live at peace with us, then we have to make difficult and even painful decisions to protect our marriage and children.

CHAPTER 3

Study Guide

for Individuals and Groups

Group leaders should prepare prior to the group meeting with the following steps:

- *Review Chapter 3.*
- *Read Romans 12:17–18.*
- *Choose one discussion question and one reflection question for group engagement in case time runs short.*
- *Pray for each group member by name. Ask the Lord to prepare their hearts and minds.*
- *If possible, silence your cell phone and remove any other distractions. Be fully present for your group and prepare to see lives transformed by God.*

Chapter 3 Summary

In this chapter we discuss 10 types of dysfunctional in-law relationships:

1. **The Bullies**
   Bullying in-laws use their power to belittle, manipulate, criticize, intimidate, and control others. They must be given

clear boundaries because without boundaries, they will inflict unmendable damage upon your marriage and family.

2. **The Judges**

Driven by the need to maintain control, judges make the rules and set the standards. They will attempt to make you and your spouse play by their self-created rules, occasionally letting you know when you have succeeded but always informing you when you have failed.

3. **The Elitists**

Elitists tend to look down on both you and others. They might subtly or obviously let you know you're lucky to be associated with their family. They may even communicate that you will never truly be part of their family.

4. **The Takers**

Takers will always try to take whatever they can get. If you have financial means, then they'll want your generosity at every turn. If you don't have a lot of money, then they'll push for other things, like access to you or time with your kids.

5. **The Scorekeepers**

Scorekeepers always keep a tally, and consequently, you will always feel as though you are losing on their scorecard even if you don't know what game is being played.

6. **The Gaslighters**

Gaslighters constantly rewrite history and redefine reality to give themselves the upper hand in relationships. They try to make anyone who disagrees with them question their own judgment, and in the worst cases, gaslighters' targets start to feel as though they are crazy.

7. **The Separators**

Separators constantly want to divide you and your spouse. Their actions show that they want to put a wedge between you and your spouse so that they can keep control over their "child" without your interference.

8. **The Smotherers**

Smotherers are usually operating out of sweet and self-less motives. But when one or both of your in-laws is a helper by nature, they may go overboard with the desire to help.

9. **The Chemically Imbalanced**

The chemically imbalanced may struggle with chemical addiction to drugs or alcohol, or they may have other physical issues that require medication. Encouraging necessary medications can be a delicate conversation and also might eventually require some sort of intervention.

10. **The Ghosts**

Ghosts intentionally vanish from your life. Contact becomes less and less frequent until you are not part of each other's lives at all anymore.

God is our source of strength, especially when our hearts are broken. He sees our pain and knows how to put the pieces back together— even if our parents, in-laws, or other loved ones act in unhealthy ways toward us. The goal is always to rebuild the relationship while also establishing healthy boundaries so that unhealthy dynamics are not perpetuated. God's plan is always reconciliation and unity whenever possible. We're called to do our part to live at peace with those in our lives.

Discussion

1. Which unhealthy type of in-laws do you find most troublesome?

2. What are some ways you have (or should) set boundaries with people who have unhealthy behaviors (whether or not they are in your family)?

3. How should you pray about unhealthy relationships so you can avoid becoming unhealthy yourself?

Reflection

1. God wants us to live at peace with others. Is there anything you are currently doing that does not promote peace?

2. How can you be more supportive of your spouse if your parents or other family members are causing disunity in your marriage?

3. What discussions do you need to have with your parents, in-laws, or spouse to increase the health of your relationships?

4. Who can you talk to about the struggles you are facing with in-laws, such as a pastor, professional Christian counselor, or Christian meditator?

Prayer

Dear Father, please help me to keep the right attitude as I relate to my parents, in-laws, and spouse. I want to be a person who promotes peace. If I have acted in ways that cause disunity, I repent of those actions and ask You to help me make things right with those I have hurt. I don't know how to fix everyone else in my life, but I know You do. Please fix me in my broken places. I ask You to work in places I cannot. But where I can do something to create better relationships, I ask Your Holy Spirit to reveal to me the actions I should take. I love my spouse and always want them to feel that I am a safe place and a refuge. Lord, make me into the kind of person my spouse can always trust. In Jesus' name, Amen.

SECTION TWO

PROTECTING MARRIAGE UNITY

Since they are no longer two but one, let no one split apart what God has joined together.

—Matthew 19:6

My wife and I have three grown children, and we have always had a close marriage and a close family. Recently, our oldest daughter married a young man whom we genuinely liked. We felt good about the match, but even though we seemed to have a good relationship with him, within the first year of their marriage, my daughter seemed to change for the worse and her husband seemed to be perpetuating this negative change. They both have started acting rudely towards us when they're not avoiding us altogether. My wife and I are on hugely different pages when it comes to how we should respond. This issue with our daughter and son-in-law is not only heartbreaking in our relationship with her, but it's also causing a great strain on our marriage. We desperately need to be unified in our response. This issue is driving a very painful wedge between us.

—Joe W. (Married 31 years)

CHAPTER 4

Defining and Setting Boundaries

I (Ashley) don't know a whole lot about sports, but I do know that certain plays in a game aren't good if the player goes out of bounds. In baseball, your pitch isn't considered good unless it is in a certain area over the plate, and a ball isn't fair unless it's inside the foul poles. In a football game, you can't score a field goal unless the football goes directly through the uprights, and when a player goes out of bounds, the play stops. Staying within the boundary lines is extremely important for a team to score or, better yet, win the game. It works the same way in our marriages.

> Healthy boundaries must be in place
> to protect our marriage and position it
> to be as strong as possible.

As a couple, we must establish boundaries to protect the integrity and health of our marriage and family. It is vital for us to be on the same page when it comes to our boundaries. Just like when we're parenting our children, we must also present a united front of established boundaries to those around us. Healthy boundaries must be in place to protect our marriage and position it to be as strong as possible.

5 Out-of-Bounds Behaviors

What boundaries or guidelines should we establish in our marriage? To answer this question, we must contemplate which acts are considered "out of bounds," especially when we are navigating rocky relationships with our in-laws. Here are *five behaviors that are out of bounds in marriage:*

1. Ignoring your spouse

Avoiding this behavior seems like an easy decision to many people, but it happens all-too-often in marriage. Some people ignore their spouse when they don't get their way as a means of punishing them. Others ignore their spouse simply to avoid talking about hard issues. Whatever the motivation, we shouldn't avoid our spouses or emotionally shut them out of our lives. When we operate this way, we break down the intimacy and leave ourselves and our spouses open to forming unhealthy habits, including the temptation to seek connection outside the marriage. You must always be willing to talk to your spouse whether you feel like it or not. You should make eye contact and connect with them because of your love and respect for your spouse. The more you do this, the stronger, healthier, and happier your marriage will be.

If your spouse comes to you with concerns about your parents, don't ignore your spouse. You might feel as if you are stuck between a rock and a hard place because you love your spouse *and* your parents. However, you must remember that the Bible teaches that your spouse deserves your first loyalty. Avoiding the issue will never solve the problem. Listen to what your spouse has to say. Don't jump to conclusions or make excuses for things your parents have done that have hurt your spouse. Remember, it might be hard to see your own parents' flaws because you have been used to living with them and adjusting to them your entire life. Be open to the possibility that you may have some blind spots that are preventing you from seeing the real issues that need to be addressed.

2. Speaking negatively about your spouse to other people, including family members

If you have an issue with your spouse, you must address the problem directly *with your spouse*. Nothing good will come from going to friends or family members about a problem that you really need to work through with your spouse. This admonition doesn't mean you avoid having people in your life you can talk to about your marriage. We just caution you over *how* you talk about your spouse and *what* you say about them to other people, especially family members.

Please understand that it is extremely hard for family members to forget negative things you tell them about your spouse. They are family, which means they are (usually) going to take your side, right or wrong. Your parents, brothers, sisters, cousins, aunts, uncles, and grandparents don't need to know all the details of every disagreement you ever have with your spouse. They especially don't need information about any major issues you are currently working through together. Marriage is hard enough without extended family drama, so don't add to the problem. If you feel as though family members could be a helpful sounding board, then be mindful of the tone you use and the words you choose if you share information about your spouse. If you are not careful, then what you thought was harmless venting (from which you quickly recover) can permanently impact your parents' or other family members' views of your spouse. It's natural for parents to want to protect their children—even their adult children—so when they hear about how your spouse hurt your feelings, let you down, or broke your trust, it's hard for them to let that go, even if you and your spouse have long since addressed the issue and moved forward. Sometimes, it is wiser and more practical for you and your spouse each to have a same-gender, non-family member as an accountability partner and sounding board.

We would like to make an important disclaimer: if you are being abused in any way, please reach out to a trusted person for help. The National Domestic Violence Hotline phone number is 800-799-7233, and their website is www.thehotline.org.

3. Allowing other people to speak negatively about your spouse

As husband and wife, we should be the *first* to protect each other's reputations. Even so, there are times when we may have problems with no easy solutions. You should never allow your family, friends, or anyone else to speak negatively about your spouse. If you have this kind of experience, then you can put to a stop to it by kindly saying, "Please don't talk about my spouse that way." It is as simple as that. If the person you are talking to won't oblige, then kindly and calmly say, "Until you can speak kindly about my spouse, I won't be able to continue this conversation" and then walk away. This response also applies to parents and in-laws. Your boundary will set a precedent, and your spouse will appreciate knowing you have their back. It is important to establish this same boundary during an intense phone conversation or text exchange. You can share the same words, and instead of walking away, gently hang up the phone or stop responding to the angry texts for a time.

4. Keeping secrets from one another

Unless you are planning a surprise party for your spouse, you have no business keeping any secrets from them. When we keep secrets of any kind from each other, we limit the amount of intimacy we can experience with our spouse. Consider each secret as a brick added to a "wall of secrets" between you and your spouse. Some bricks might be bigger than others, but all secrets are the building blocks for the wall. There should be no barricade between a husband and a wife. There should be no secret money, friends, texts, emails, letters, jobs, purchases, phone calls, phones, social media exchanges, social media accounts, health issues, trips, outings, lunches, dinners, or anything else. If you keep secrets from your spouse, even if they are between you and your family members, you are in dangerous territory. In fact, when we have worked with couples having in-law difficulties that infringe on their marriages, most of these spouses have cited secrets between in-laws and their spouses as major trust-killers. You may think of these secrets as harmless, but there is no room for secrets between a husband and a wife. No good comes from it. If your parents are constantly telling you to keep something from your spouse, then that is a huge red flag, and you must address it. The next time someone asks you to keep a secret from your spouse, simply tell them that you don't keep anything from your spouse because you are one—you are united. If they don't like your response and tell you that it's weird or it makes them trust you less, then say something such as,

> Well, I am sorry that is how you feel. We both love you so much, and we hope you know that you can trust us—both of us. However, if you don't want my spouse to know about something, then you shouldn't tell me about that particular thing. I hope you understand.

Any person asking you to keep secrets from your spouse is undermining your spouse's character, coming between you and your spouse, and indirectly affecting your own trust in your spouse.

Any person asking you to keep secrets from your spouse is undermining your spouse's character, coming between you and your spouse, and indirectly affecting your own trust in your spouse. Odds are your family member isn't actively trying to come between you and your spouse by asking you to keep secrets. They just want to keep a close relationship with you. Some people see shared secrets as a sign of intimacy or closeness. Even so, keeping family secrets from your spouse will negatively affect your intimacy and connection, and it will cause your spouse to be suspicious and untrusting of your family member(s).

5. Speaking unkindly or shouting at one another

Every married couple is going to disagree at some point, and there will be times when an argument ensues. It is healthier to go ahead and talk through a disagreement than it is to hold it inside and let it fester. However, it is not okay to speak in a nasty tone, use harsh language, or scream and shout at one another. It's hard to forget hateful things that are said to us. We don't have a license to give our spouses a tongue-lashing. In fact, we made a promise to love our spouses through the good times and the bad times.

Lashing out at each other is not loving one another. Always do your best to approach a disagreement with your spouse as calmly and lovingly as possible. It may be especially difficult when you are facing in-law issues because tensions are high. For those whose parents seem to be the cause of the friction, it can feel like you are in a no-win situation, and more often than not, you end up unleashing this frustration at home. This intense conflict is counterproductive and can also be damaging to your marriage.

Instead of becoming overwhelmed and lashing out at your spouse, talk as calmly as possible about how you are feeling. You should also ask your partner how they are feeling and really listen to what they have to say. Remember, you and your spouse are on the same team. As teammates who want to win together, you must constructively work together and steer clear of unproductive and potentially damaging behaviors that are out of bounds. Then the two of you can have the same goal as you work to establish healthy boundaries with your parents and in-laws.

Discovering the Necessary Boundaries

Families are messy. Even the healthiest ones experience occasional forms of tension, drama, and brokenness. We are often blind to our own family's flaws because whatever we experienced growing up feels very "normal" to us. Once we get married and a new person enters our family system, their outside perspective can start to shine a light on the dysfunction we've grown accustomed to.

Dealing with those uncomfortable realities that are exposed during a marriage's early days can cause a great deal of tension for couples. Even the healthiest marriages experience some "culture clash" because of their different upbringings and family value systems. This unexpected tension happened to our friends Rob and Tracey.

Rob grew up in an upper middle-class suburb where his dad was a respected pediatrician, and his mom was a volunteer leader at the school and in their family's church. In addition to his lucrative doctor's salary, Rob's dad inherited a lot of wealth from his parents, so the family never experienced any form of financial need or scarcity. Rob was a star athlete in school and had one younger sister who made stellar grades and was successful in local beauty pageants. On the surface, everything seemed perfect in their family. Tracey's first impression was that Rob's family was very rich and picture perfect in every way.

Tracey's family, on the other hand, had always struggled financially. She was born out of wedlock and had never known her biological father. Her mom and stepdad married when she was two years old, and he became the only father she had ever known. He had always been a great dad to her. Tracey had two younger brothers who both planned to continue in the family's plumbing business. Her dad was a plumber while her mom had stayed at home to homeschool the kids. Tracey had a happy home life. She never went without any of her basic needs being met, but from Rob's perspective, her family was sweet but lacking resources.

Rob loved Tracey's family, but he thought they were too controlling over her. In his eyes, Tracey's parents expected her to follow a strict set of rules and guidelines even though she was an adult. Having been homeschooled, Tracey had lived in a very controlled environment. Rob appreciated the genuine warmth and affection in their family home, but he secretly thought the family was backward, simple-minded, and legalistic.

Tracey loved Rob's family, but she had always felt a little judged by them. Rob's mom liked to make subtle (and sometimes not-so-subtle) comments about Tracey's family being from a "rougher" part of town. She also made jokes about plumbers and talked about Tracey's blue-collar upbringing. Rob's mom even referred to Tracey's dad as her "stepfather," even though Tracey clearly called him "Dad" and had always known him as such. Rob's mom also assumed that all holiday traditions and scheduling conflicts would be accommodated by Tracey's family since Rob's dad had an "important job" and couldn't change his schedule. At first, Tracey had felt loved and accepted by Rob's family, but with each passive aggressive remark and careless assumption, she began feeling more and more isolated and disrespected. Rob seemed blind to his mom's little digs at Tracy and her family. Even when Tracey pointed out specific examples of the behavior, Rob just dismissed the issue, which made Tracey feel unheard by her husband.

Tracey also started to see some unhealthy behaviors in Rob's family culture that she hadn't noticed before. While the family had always worked hard to display a picture-perfect image wherever they went, Tracey saw the inner workings of the family structure and knew there was some trouble in their so-called paradise. Rob's parents didn't appear to have a good marriage, and their schedules showed a pattern of avoiding each other as much as possible. Rob's dad was either working or playing golf. His mom stayed busy too. Rob's sister felt neglected by both parents. She was running on a performance treadmill, always working to appease her parents by receiving good grades or turning heads with her good looks. It seemed obvious to Tracey that both parents favored Rob over his sister, and behind his sister's beautiful smile, there was a brokenhearted girl who always longed for her parents' approval. The family's value system seemed to be based on superficial criteria rather than unconditional love. The family seemed to have a persistent urgency for things to appear healthy instead of a desire for things to actually be healthy. The only time the family seemed to be completely honest or show any real affection with each other was when they were drinking alcohol, which happened a lot. This drinking dynamic was also new to Tracey because she had grown up in a household where drinking alcohol was frowned upon.

One of the most important priorities for Rob and Tracey was that their own marriage and future family would be built on a foundation of faith in God along with participation in the local church. Both Rob's family and Tracey's family went to the same megachurch, which was really the only place these families' lives overlapped. Rob and Tracey met in the church's youth group. While it was a comfort to both families that their kids had found someone who shared their faith, the daily expression of that faith looked drastically different.

In-Law Relationship Questions

Tension around issues related to their parents marked the early years of Rob and Tracey's marriage. They had to confront some of the same tough questions most couples must address, such as:

- How do we honor the legacies of both families yet create our own unique legacy?

- How do we honor both families' values when parts of the value systems seem broken?

- Which parts of our individual upbringings do we want to transfer to our own family and children? Which aspects do we never want to carry on?

- How will we defend each other if one of our parents or relatives shows disrespect or becomes controlling over our lives or the lives of our children?

- How can we build a strong, lifelong bond with our parents while we maintain healthy boundaries that protect our marriage and family?

- How should we divide our time and holidays between both families in a way that seems fair and balanced? How will we defend our choices if challenged?

- How can we offer helpful critiques about some parts of each other's upbringings without coming across as disrespectful or judgmental toward our respective families?

- What does it mean for us to "leave and cleave" as the Bible teaches? Will it require us to move away from our families so we can build a strong marriage and family of our own?

- How much help can or should we give if a parent or relative needs physical or financial support?

- How can we support a healthy relationship between our kids and our parents even if we have a strained relationship with our parents?

- As our own children get married and we become the "in-laws," how should we nurture healthy behaviors and avoid unhealthy ones?

- What should we do to build a healthy, multi-generational legacy that includes faith, love, and shared values?

We encourage you to talk with your spouse about each of these important questions. Be prepared for multiple conversations. In fact, a healthy approach is to return to them occasionally for reassessment. Married couples often need to monitor and adjust expectations, boundaries, and approaches as they grow and learn about marriage, themselves, and their in-laws.

Boundary Questions

Once you have gone through each in-law relationship question, work toward agreement on boundaries you would like to set up. Again, these may shift a bit during different seasons, but it is good to create a flexible framework that will keep your marriage strong and your in-law relationships healthy. Consider these following questions to help you establish boundaries:

- How many days a week do we need to touch base with our parents?

- Once we agree on frequency, how can we achieve it? Do we make phone calls, send texts, organize family dinners, or plan visits? What will be our mix?

- What is the biggest concern we have with our parents now?

- What steps can we take to ease some feelings of tension for both us and our parents? Can we make some schedule changes? Would an honest conversation to directly address the issues help? Should we consider spending a little less time with our parents in the short term? Do we need to make any apologies? How can we offer forgiveness even if no apology has been offered?

- Do we feel that our parents are disregarding any of our boundaries? If so, what is the best way for us to address this issue with them? Should we call, send a text, or sit down and discuss the issue over a meal? Should one or both of us address the boundary issue? Which would be most effective and lead to a healthier relationship?

- Have either of us crossed our parents' boundaries? If so, how should we discuss the issue with them and make it right?

These questions will go a long way to help you as a couple drill down to the nitty gritty issue of boundaries. Make sure to have these conversations with the right spirit—don't let them become bash-fests where you only express frustration. That is easy to do when tensions are high. Instead, concentrate on the current state of your relationships and how you would like to improve them. Focus on the actions you and your spouse should take to improve the health of your marriage and your other family relationships.

Navigating Disagreements

God wants married couples to live in unity, but unity does *not* always mean unanimity or uniformity. Husbands and wives should be unified in their mutual commitment to each other and their core convictions. However, because you are two different people, you will have different perspectives, opinions, and personalities, which will lead to some disagreements.

When differences arise, how should we respond? That may seem like a loaded question, and it is because there are no one-size-fits-all answers. Every situation is unique. For example, if your spouse wants to become an illicit drug dealer and put the entire family at risk, then you have a responsibility to disagree without compromise. But on the other end of the continuum, perhaps your spouse wants to watch a TV show you think is boring. Instead of staging an intervention and stealing the remote, you might consider serving them by allowing them to have their preference without protest. If we allow selfish pride to creep into our disagreements, then the lack of unity may destroy peace, erode trust, and eventually end the marriage altogether.

Three Categories of Disagreements

To help you understand the variety of potential disagreements you might have in your relationship with your spouse, we are going to list three categories along with the primary goal for each of them. There are exceptions, of course, and there may be other types of disagreements, but we have found that most marital issues fit into one of these categories:

1. **Principle issues**

2. **Preference issues**

3. **Poisonous issues**

Principle Issues

Principle issues include commitments, such as those to each other, to your children, to a core set of values, or to having healthy in-law relationships. These issues are so foundational to a marriage that a disagreement becomes tantamount to divorce and may lead to one. In areas of principle, you must fight for the unity of your marriage. Even if your opinions differ slightly over how you should live out principle commitments, you must find agreement over the "main things" and be uncompromisingly unified on them going forward.

> You must find agreement over the "main things" and be uncompromisingly unified on them going forward.

Preference Issues

Preference issues refer to those everyday matters, big and small, that largely come down to personal inclination. We estimate that at least 90 percent of all marriage decisions fall under this category of issues. Examples include what house to purchase, what color to paint a wall, what food to eat for dinner, and what name to give to each child. Spouses must share input toward these decisions, but they will not always agree. In times of disagreement, seek out ways to serve your spouse by allowing their preference whenever possible.

Note that this same rule does not apply when you have disagreements with people outside your marriage, which includes your in-laws. In times like those, all family members should make their preferences known but also be willing to bend a little. Each person must understand that families consist of multiple people with a variety of perspectives and preferences, and keeping the peace often requires some compromise along with putting some personal preferences aside for the greater good of family unity.

If your spouse, parents, or in-laws rarely (or never) reciprocate by yielding to your or another person's preferences, then you could be dealing with a bully or a narcissist, which requires a different level of interaction. In those cases, you will have to establish and maintain some specific, healthy boundaries for the sake of your marriage and family. Setting boundaries can be challenging because bullies and narcissists will always believe their way is best. They shun compromise and refuse to bend. However, if you allow a bully or narcissist to win constantly, then you only contribute to worsening the problem. Establishing healthy boundaries and being consistent to keep them is imperative for the good of your marriage and family.[1]

Poisonous Issues

Poisonous issues include matters of sin, secrecy, and deceit in a marriage. These issues can bring about financial recklessness, sexual infidelity, drug addiction, law-breaking, and a host of other complications. They have the potential to inflict irreparable harm on the entire family. A spouse living in intentional sin might pridefully insist that their toxic actions do not impact anyone else, but their sin has a direct and devastating impact on the other spouse and the entire family. When these reckless behaviors start to happen, you should not sit by and hope they go away. Your silence implies your approval. Instead, you must intervene to make sure the behavior stops as you protect everyone else in the family.

These same principles apply when addressing issues with our parents and in-laws. If a family member consistently attends family functions under the influence of alcohol or drugs, always expects others to pick up the bill at a restaurant, tries to get other family members engaged in illegal activity, or demands that other family members ignore toxic behavior, then you are dealing with poisonous family issues. You must address the situation sooner rather than later. As always, confront the family member honestly and directly but also with love. These kinds of confrontations often require the aid of a professional Christian mediator or counselor.

After you have addressed a poisonous issue, you can help your loved one get the help they need. Some solutions include urging them to go to a substance abuse recovery center, insisting on separate checks at restaurants, or encouraging them to accept responsibility for illegal actions. While your loved one is healing (or until they seek help), you must maintain healthy boundaries to protect your own mental health and marriage. Practically speaking, your boundaries might consist of not allowing your children to be around a family member with substance abuse issues until that person is sober and actively seeking recovery. You might have to explain that you don't feel like they are "safe" people because they participate in illegal activities. For the sake and safety of your own family, you can't be around them until they stop the illegal behavior. Remember, the goal is always reconciliation and restoration whenever possible, so keeping an open line of communication is key, even if you must establish boundaries that keep you from being in their physical presence for a season.

God's Word for Family Issues

Dealing with toxic family issues is not for the faint of heart, but we serve a God who is greater than any mountain before us. Do not lose hope. Remember, He is always with you and for you! Keep your mind and heart soft and focused on the good things God is doing in your life and in the lives of your family members. Consistently pray and memorize verses such as these:

> Dealing with toxic family issues is not for the faint of heart, but we serve a God who is greater than any mountain before us.

A soft answer turns away wrath,
    but a harsh word stirs up anger (Proverbs 15:1 ESV).

Finally, brothers and sisters, whatever is true, whatever is noble, whatever is right, whatever is pure, whatever is lovely, whatever is admirable—if anything is excellent or praiseworthy—think about such things (Philippians 4:8 NIV).

Let your speech always be gracious, seasoned with salt, so that you may know how you ought to answer each person (Colossians 4:6 ESV).

The LORD is my chosen portion and my cup;
  you hold my lot.
The lines have fallen for me in pleasant places;
  indeed, I have a beautiful inheritance.
I bless the LORD who gives me counsel;
  in the night also my heart instructs me.
I have set the LORD always before me;
  because he is at my right hand, I shall not be shaken.
Therefore my heart is glad, and my whole being rejoices;
  my flesh also dwells secure (Psalm 16:5–9 ESV).

Therefore be imitators of God, as beloved children. And walk in love, as Christ loved us and gave himself up for us, a fragrant offering and sacrifice to God. But sexual immorality and all impurity or covetousness must not even be named among you, as is proper among saints. Let there be no filthiness nor foolish talk nor crude joking, which are out of place, but instead let there be thanksgiving (Ephesians 5:1–4 ESV).

For I do not mean that others should be eased and you burdened, but that as a matter of fairness your abundance at the present time should supply their need, so that their abundance may supply your need, that there may be fairness (2 Corinthians 8:13–14 ESV).

———————

The LORD is near to the brokenhearted
   and saves the crushed in spirit (Psalm 34:18 ESV).

———————

Fear not, for I am with you;
   be not dismayed, for I am your God;
I will strengthen you, I will help you,
   I will uphold you with my righteous right hand
   (Isaiah 41:10 ESV).

Same Team Mentality

Over the years, we have received thousands of marriage-related questions about almost every conceivable topic. We have gotten questions about sex, money, communication, parenting, navigating disagreements, rebuilding trust, in-laws, and countless other topics. Of all the questions we receive, one of the most common is, "What is your all-time favorite marriage advice?"

It's a really great question but also a difficult one for us to answer. We believe there many important nuggets of marriage advice, including these:

- Put Jesus first.
- Talk about everything.
- Be honest.
- Be patient.

- Be loving.
- Make sure you are prioritizing time together.

All of those are great pieces of marriage advice, but we have one more thing we consistently share that seems to get people's attention more than any of the others. When we share it, we watch as people pause, raise their eyebrows, and then say, "Wow. I've never thought about it that way before."

Here's that *one* piece of advice: **You and your spouse are on the *same team*. It's never him against her or her against him. You're in this together.** As we say this, we mean that in every disagreement there won't be a "winner" and a "loser." Since you're on the same team, you'll either win together or lose together. Work together to find solutions through which you'll both win. Fight for and not against each other, and never forget you're on the same team!

> You and your spouse are on the *same team*. It's never him against her or her against him. You're in this together.

This advice might sound too simple to some people, but most of the best marriage advice is really very simple. Humans tend to overcomplicate things and lose sight of that which is clear and plain. We start out instinctively knowing we're in marriage together and on the same team, but then life's stresses and circumstances cloud our vision, and we miss the main point of marriage.

If you are struggling for the unity you once had in your marriage, then call a "team meeting." Apologize to each other and to God. Then create a game plan to get back on the right track. No matter what's been said or done, healing is possible. You can do this! Do not settle for living as strangers, roommates, or rivals. Live as partners, lovers, and best friends.

Return to the team. Start cheering for each other again instead of criticizing. Give each other more high fives and fewer eye rolls. Be willing to apologize for anything you have done to contribute to the current brokenness and be willing to forgive your spouse for their mistakes. Let your words, your actions, and even the tone of your voice communicate this clear message: "I'm with you. I am for you. I love you, and I'll always be on your team."

When it comes to your principles, fight for unity. With issues of preference, celebrate unity within your diversity. As you deal with poisonous issues, demand accountability. In all things, let love lead the way. As you work to craft your family's unified vision and culture, start with love and commitment to God and to each other. When you do this, you will always be heading in the right direction.

CHAPTER 4

Study Guide

for Individuals and Groups

Group leaders should prepare prior to the group meeting with the following steps:

- *Review Chapter 4.*

- *Read Psalm 34:18; Proverbs 15:1; and Isaiah 41:10.*

- *Choose one discussion question and one reflection question for group engagement in case time runs short.*

- *Pray for each group member by name. Ask the Lord to prepare their hearts and minds.*

- *If possible, silence your cell phone and remove any other distractions. Be fully present for your group and prepare to see lives transformed by God.*

Chapter 4 Summary

As a couple, we must establish boundaries to protect the integrity and health of our marriage and family. It is vital for us to be on the same page when it comes to our boundaries.

Here are *five behaviors that are out of bounds in marriage:*

1. Ignoring your spouse

2. Speaking negatively about your spouse to other people, including family members

3. Allowing other people to speak negatively about your spouse

4. Keeping secrets from one another

5. Speaking unkindly or shouting at one another

Families are messy. Even the healthiest ones experience occasional forms of tension, drama, and brokenness. We are often blind to our own family's flaws because whatever we experienced growing up feels very "normal" to us. Once we get married and a new person enters our family system, their outside perspective can start to shine a light on the dysfunction we've grown accustomed to.

We encourage you to talk with your spouse about the important in-law questions listed in this chapter, followed by the boundaries questions. Be prepared for multiple conversations. In fact, a healthy approach is to return to these questions occasionally for reassessment. Married couples often need to monitor and adjust expectations, boundaries, and approaches as they grow and learn about marriage, themselves, and their in-laws.

Most marital issues fit into one of these three types of disagreements:

1. **Principle issues**: commitments, such as those to each other, to your children, to a core set of values, or to having healthy in-law relationships

2. **Preference issues**: everyday matters, big and small, that largely come down to personal inclination

3. **Poisonous issues**: matters of sin, secrecy, and deceit in a marriage

Dealing with toxic family issues is not for the faint of heart, but we serve a God who is greater than any mountain before us. Do not lose hope. Remember, He is always with you and for you! His Word is full of promises for you, your spouse, and your family.

Our all-time favorite marriage advice is this: **You and your spouse are on the *same team*. It's never him against her or her against him. You are in this together.** Work together to find solutions through which you'll both win. Fight for and not against each other, and never forget you're on the same team!

Discussion

1. Have you realized you need clearer boundaries in your marriage? If so, what event(s) led you to this conclusion?

2. As you review the five out-of-bounds behaviors, which of these have been present in your marriage? Are they still present, and if so, how do you plan to address them?

3. As you read about the three major categories of disagreements, which of these has most plagued your relationship?

Reflection

1. How will you address the out-of-bounds behaviors in your relationship?

2. How would you respond to a couple who told you they are struggling to establish boundaries with their families?

3. When you think about your relationship with your in-laws, what are some boundaries you know you need to set to improve your relationship?

4. How can you show your spouse that you are on the same team?

Prayer

Father God, sometimes I struggle with setting boundaries, either because of confusion or fear. Help me to have a clear mind and heart as I do what is necessary to protect my marriage. I want to show my spouse that we are on the same team. I ask You to show me how to turn disunity into unity. Forgive me for the times I have not been in unity with my spouse, and help me as I acknowledge and apologize for those behaviors. Even more than that, show me the areas of my life where I have not been in unity with You. I want to make you my top priority. I know if I do that, then You will show me how to make my spouse a priority too. I always want to stand for You and my spouse. Please help me. In Jesus name, Amen.

CHAPTER 5

Shared Family Events and Holidays

Corinne and Mike have been married for eight years. They have two young kids, and overall, they have an incredibly happy life together. Their family isn't perfect, but it is joyful. To be more accurate, everything is great *until the holiday season hits.* Their marriage is mostly happy from January until mid-November, but then the weeks leading up to Thanksgiving all the way through Christmas make everything and everyone tense and intense.

Does Corrine and Mike's relationship sound peculiar? Why would their marriage start unraveling at the same time Christmas decorations start appearing? Aren't the year-end holidays supposed to be the most wonderful time of the year? Why would the very sight of Santa Claus put this couple on guard and make them ready for a fight?

Corinne and Mike's annual drama is rooted in their rocky relationships with their parents and in-laws. Like many other couples, the tension in their family relationships increases around the holidays. When Thanksgiving and Christmas draw close, the good things in life seem even better, but the hard things feel even more difficult. Everything—the good, the bad, and the ugly—is amplified!

For Corinne and Mike, family tension started when they were still newlyweds. Corrine's mother had a domineering personality and always insisted on keeping her own holiday traditions uninterrupted. After Corinne married, there was another family to consider, but her mother could not see it that way. Mike had a family of peacemakers who would bend over backwards to accommodate everyone else around holidays, but years later, all that peacemaking felt like it had only "fed the beast," enabling Corinne's mom to continue operating without accountability.

Through the years, the couple had spent increasingly more time with Corinne's parents around the holidays, but it never seemed to be enough to satisfy Corinne's mom. Corinne's dad was a generally reasonable man, but he desperately wanted to keep the peace in his own home, so he had never mustered the courage to stand up to his wife or point out her unfair demands. While Mike's family continued to be overwhelmingly accommodating, Corinne's mom made the outrageously flippant and untrue claim that the holiday schedule should remain unchanged because "Mike's family doesn't have any traditions."

Mike's family remained very patient despite the selfish demands and insults coming from Corinne's mom, but they began to be deeply hurt by the imbalance. They felt as though their own family traditions were being held hostage by Corinne's family, particularly her mother. Mike's family started to express resentment because of the whole scenario. Whenever a new holiday season started to roll around, members of both Mike and Corinne's families started feeling defensive.

While they love their families, Mike and Corinne started to despise the holidays. They began to see the holidays as an ordeal to *survive* rather than a pleasure to celebrate. Corinne felt stuck in the middle and triangulated. She felt deep sadness as though she was always letting someone down. Mike also felt resentful as he recognized how his family had been cheated in the annual holiday games. Overall, everyone felt exhausted and simply wanted the holidays to be over with so they could get back to normal. However, even as January rolled around again, the impending dread of the next year's celebrations set in.

While we focus on the time between Thanksgiving and Christmas in this chapter, many of these principles can apply to other family events, such as Easter, birthdays, the Fourth of July, vacations, or any other times when families gather. We share this story because scenarios very much like Mike and Corinne's are played out in many homes. It is a common in-law dilemma. Most couples want their in-law relationships to be healthy, yet sometimes the tension never seems to end. There's only a brief lull until it starts all over again the next time. This impasse boils down to a few key questions every married couple must confront:

- How do we honor our parents during the holidays while maintaining healthy boundaries that protect our marriage?

- How can we become peacemakers within our respective families of origin without cowering to the most dominant personalities or enabling those who exhibit unhealthy behaviors?

- How can we ensure unity within our own marriage while we build healthy multigenerational bonds with both sides of our families, especially around special celebrations?

- How can we find balance and maintain fairness as we make an effort to see both sides of our families while still establishing and protecting our own new holiday traditions?

In our own marriage, we haven't been immune to some holiday family tensions. Both sets of parents and siblings live in the same area, and we're the only ones who have moved away. When we come back to our hometown for the holidays, we sometimes feel like a ping pong ball bouncing back and forth. We do our best to please everyone, but we don't always succeed. We love our families, but there's simply not enough time to see everyone as much as we or they would like.

Whenever you run into complicated holiday scenarios, our advice for you and couples like Mike and Corinne comes from our own experience of navigating troubled holiday waters year after year. We can't give you a perfect formula for family harmony, but we have learned these principles that have helped us and made the holidays fun again:

- Realize you're not going to please everybody (and that's okay).

- Try your best to find a balance between how much time you're spending with each family but be sure to give yourselves grace. It will never be exactly even, and that's also okay.

- Honor your parents, but remember that honoring them as married adults doesn't mean obeying them or doing everything they want in the same way you did when you were children. Sometimes you might have to disappoint them in the most honoring, respectful, and loving way you possibly can.

- Try your best to be fully present wherever you are. Instead of thinking about rushing to the next group of people, focus on relaxing and engaging with the people and activities that are happening right in front of you.

- Understand that God has called you to be a peacemaker but *not* a doormat.

God has called you to be a peacemaker but *not* a doormat.

- If you're traveling and need your own space, don't feel bad about booking a hotel room rather than staying in a family member's home. In fact, this choice might be better for your family too, even though they won't admit it.

- Make sure you're working to secure moments to connect as a couple even while you try to connect with your relatives.

- Don't spend money you don't have buying gifts. Stick to a budget and check your motives. Don't use money to try to win favor with your family.

- Do your best to let your kids experience Christmas morning in your own home. Don't feel bad about establishing your own family holiday traditions.

- Even amidst the chaos and commercialism that often accompany the holiday season, take time to refocus your mind on what these days are all about: thankfulness, joy, peace, love, and, most of all, Jesus.

Marriage Lessons from Mary and Joseph

As we close out this chapter discussing our family relationships during the holidays, we want to turn your attention to the most important Christmas story of all—the very first one. If you're like most people, whenever you think of Joseph and Mary, you probably visualize figurines in a Nativity set or think about images adorning the front of Christmas cards. Our thoughts of Joseph and Mary are inextricably linked to the story of Jesus' birth. While His coming into the world as a baby is obviously a moment of immeasurable significance, if we only view Mary and Joseph through the lens of that one night, then we will miss out on some very important lessons they can teach us about marriage.

As a husband and wife who speak and write about marriage issues almost daily, we've always been fascinated by Joseph and Mary as a married couple. Their relationship is captured in the first few chapters of the Gospels of Matthew and Luke, and their example proves to be one of the healthiest models for marriage recorded anywhere in the Bible. We believe that if we can see beyond the artificial plastic figures in Christmas decorations and see them in light of their faith, humanity, and love for God and each other, then our own lives and marriages can be enriched as a result.

We don't have much information about their in-law dynamics, but we know enough from historical and cultural backgrounds and the biblical witness to understand that Mary's out-of-wedlock pregnancy greatly complicated the circumstances surrounding their new marriage. We overlook something important if we only focus on their roles as Jesus' parents at Christmas and forget the powerful witness of their marriage that we can follow all year long. Mary and Joseph provide a healthy example for marriage and family even in the few Bible passages that tell their story. Here are *three positive lessons* about marriage from the biblical account that you can apply to your own marriage and family:

1. They worked for unity in their marriage.

From the time they were married, Joseph and Mary always appear together in the Bible. Even before their marriage, Joseph showed his commitment to Mary by protecting her and her reputation. When Joseph found out she was pregnant, it must have been an awful shock. He had already committed to marry her, and they were in the middle of the betrothal process. That means they had already publicly declared they were a couple, which was legally and ceremonially binding. They hadn't lived in the same house together yet, but there was no going back. Mary couldn't send back an engagement ring and end the betrothal without major repercussions. Joseph had not yet heard from the angel that Mary's pregnancy was an act of God. The only logical conclusion he could draw was that she had been unfaithful.

Under the Law of Moses, someone who committed adultery was put to death by stoning. Even before an angel visited Joseph, he did not want Mary to be harmed. Of course, he knew this baby was not his, but he didn't try to accuse Mary or make a public spectacle of her. In a way, Joseph covered for her because he was unwilling to expose her shame.

> Joseph, to whom she was engaged, was a righteous man and did not want to disgrace her publicly, so he decided to break the engagement quietly (Matthew 1:19).

Sometimes when we think about the word "righteous," we might think of someone who follows the "letter" of the law, but that is not the case with Joseph. He didn't want Mary to be exposed to ridicule, public contempt, or even death. Joseph was going to handle the situation as quietly as possible. He didn't want Mary to be harmed or humiliated. Joseph was a righteous, just, and good man.

Matthew explains in his Gospel that an angel appeared in a dream to Joseph (see Matthew 1:20–23). The angel told Joseph not to be afraid because the baby Mary carried was not conceived by another man but by the Holy Spirit. The visit from the angel convinced Joseph, and he took Mary into his home.

Joseph protected his wife. He did not put her out or put her down. He was concerned not only about her safety but also about her feelings. Joseph even defended her to his and her families. Holidays present us with a prime time to protect our spouses and their feelings. Sometimes families accept slights and insults as "normal," but they are *not* normal. Joseph covered for Mary out of faith, but it's also a matter of faith not to embarrass your spouse or let them be ridiculed in front of others. For example, if you were to say, "My spouse didn't really want to come today," then you aren't protecting them or their feelings. What you are saying might be true, but it helps no one. Protect your spouse. Joseph mastered this task.

When the Roman emperor demanded a census, Mary and Joseph journeyed together to Bethlehem. They were together in the stable when Jesus was born and when they dedicated their new baby at the Temple. Mary and Joseph escaped together to Egypt and returned together to Israel. They were together when they lost Jesus in the Temple compound when He was 12 years old and together when they found him. Like Joseph and Mary, your marriage will be stronger when you and your spouse choose to face everything together, even if that includes tough in-law relationships.

2. They trusted God, and they trusted each other.

Before they were married, an angel appeared to both Joseph and
Mary with the message that God was sending Jesus. After they
were married, on the two occasions when God needed to send an
important message, He only told Joseph. Joseph had to trust God,
and Mary had to trust her husband. In marriage, sometimes God
might give a vision to just one spouse, and you need to trust each
other enough for *both* of you to accept the call. Mary trusted God
that she would give birth to the Messiah, even though she was a
virgin. Joseph trusted God that he should still wed Mary, a woman
who was pregnant with a child who wasn't biologically his and
start out their marriage as a stepfather in a time where blended
families were not generally supported. Like Joseph and Mary, your
marriage will be able to overcome any obstacle when you choose
to have unshakeable faith in both God and your spouse.

Like Joseph and Mary, your marriage won't
be defined by the size of your struggles
but by the size of your commitment
to God and each other.

3. They faced hardships with faith and perseverance.

Mary and Joseph were in the center of God's will, yet they faced
difficulty in nearly every area of their lives. They likely dealt with
poverty, social ostracism for an out-of-wedlock pregnancy, a stable
as their maternity ward, running for the life of their newborn to a
foreign country to escape Herod's tyranny, and relocating to a new
community once they moved back to Israel. They never had it easy,
but their marriage was strong because they faced every challenge
together, and they trusted God completely. Like Joseph and Mary,
your marriage won't be defined by the size of your struggles but by
the size of your commitment to God and each other.

———————

There is much about Joseph and Mary's marriage and family that we don't know. The Bible does tell us, however, that Joseph and Mary had more children after the birth of Jesus. In fact, Jesus' brother James became a great leader within the early church and wrote the book of James in the New Testament. We know Joseph was a carpenter by trade, and Jesus followed in Joseph's footsteps. We also know that Joseph most likely died when Jesus was young, because Mary was a widow by the time of Jesus' recorded ministry, which began when Jesus was around 30 years of age. While there are many details about Joseph and Mary's lives that we don't know, we know enough to learn some powerful lessons from their examples.

Next time you see Joseph and Mary depicted in Christmas decorations, pause a moment to remember these were real people with real faith who had a real marriage. Just as God called Mary and Joseph to a very special work, He is also calling you and your spouse to an important mission. Like Joseph and Mary, you and your spouse will only be able to fulfill your mission for life and marriage when you choose to have faith in God and in each other.

———————

Every family dynamic is different, but the simple principles we shared in this chapter are a good starting point to help you in nearly every family situation. If you'll work to keep unity in your marriage and strive to put these principles into practice, then the holidays can once again be a time of celebration rather than tension. We pray your next holiday will be the best yet for you and your family as you start some new, healthy, and sustainable traditions that will enable you to look forward to the holidays year after year.

Study Guide

for Individuals and Groups

Group leaders should prepare prior to the group meeting with the following steps:

- *Review Chapter 5.*

- *Read Matthew 1:18–2:23.*

- *Choose one discussion question and one reflection question for group engagement in case time runs short.*

- *Pray for each group member by name. Ask the Lord to prepare their hearts and minds.*

- *If possible, silence your cell phone and remove any other distractions. Be fully present for your group and prepare to see lives transformed by God.*

Chapter 5 Summary

The holidays present a common in-law dilemma. Most couples want their in-law relationships to be healthy, yet sometimes the tension never seems to end. There's only a brief lull until it starts all over again the next time. Couples must be creative to find ways to honor their parents during the holidays while maintaining healthy boundaries that protect their marriage.

Whenever you run into complicated holiday scenarios, our advice is the following:

- Realize you are not going to please everybody (and that is okay).

- Try your best to find a balance between how much time you are spending with each family but give yourselves grace. It will never be exactly even, and that is also okay.

- Honor your parents but remember that honoring them as married adults does not mean obeying them or doing everything they want in the same way you did when you were children. Sometimes you might have to disappoint them in the most honoring, respectful, and loving way you possibly can.

- Try your best to be fully present wherever you are. Instead of thinking about rushing to the next group of people, focus on relaxing and engaging with the people and activities that are happening right in front of you.

- Understand that God has called you to be a peacemaker but *not* a doormat.

- If you are traveling and need your own space, don't feel bad about booking a hotel room rather than staying in a family member's home. In fact, this choice might be better for your family too, even though they will not admit it.

- Make sure you are working to secure moments to connect as a couple even while you try to connect with your relatives.

- Don't spend money you don't have buying gifts. Stick to a budget and check your motives. Do not use money to try to win favor with your family.

- Do your best to let your kids experience Christmas morning in your own home. Don't feel bad about establishing your own family holiday traditions.

- Even amidst the chaos and commercialism that often accompany the holiday season, take time to refocus your mind on what these days are all about: thankfulness, joy, peace, love, and, most of all, Jesus.

Mary and Joseph provide a healthy example for marriage and family even in the few Bible passages that tell their story. They worked for the unity of their marriage. They trusted God and each other, and they faced every hardship with faith and perseverance. Just as God called Mary and Joseph to a very special work, He is also calling you and your spouse to an important mission. Like Joseph and Mary, you and your spouse will only be able to fulfill your mission for life and marriage when you choose to have faith in God and in each other.

Discussion

1. What are the greatest challenges you and your spouse have faced related to the holidays?

2. Which of these challenges were related to family members, including in-laws?

3. What advice do you find most helpful for your situation? What advice would you share with newly married couples?

Reflection

1. What events during your childhood and growing up years have influenced how you experience holidays as an adult?

2. How will you decide where you will spend the holidays or how much time you will spend with each family member?

3. What parts of the holidays bring you the greatest joy? What is the greatest challenge?

4. As you read about the story of Mary and Joseph, how does hearing about the challenges they faced encourage you in your marriage?

Prayer

Father God, thank You for sending Your Son, Jesus. I want to remember that His coming to earth is the greatest part of the Christmas season. Amid all the family struggles that might arise during this time of year, help me to remember the most important event is that You came to save me. I want my spouse and children to have great experiences and memories with all holidays, so please give me wisdom to make this time the best it can be. Help my spouse and me make the right plan relating to our families during the holiday seasons. We want to honor them. Please show us the best way to do it. Thank You again for being our greatest gift. In Jesus' name, Amen.

CHAPTER 6

Difficult Conversations

Jamal and Leah came from quite different backgrounds, but they were best friends and deeply in love. They were convinced that their cultures, backgrounds, and personality differences would not cause division in their marriage. And on those particular issues, they were indeed united. So when division crept into their relationship, they were blindsided.

Jamal and Leah genuinely loved each other's families, and everyone seemed to get along. Both sides gave support from the very beginning. Jamal and Leah never dreamed that issues over in-laws would cause strife in their marriage, and they never could have expected the way all these issues would be set into motion.

It all started when Jamal's youngest sister, Maya, developed a drug addiction. She had always been an exceptional student and a loving person who made great decisions, but her life started to unravel after she experienced the trauma of a date rape from a young man she had known and trusted for years. Maya immediately reported the crime, but the prosecutor declined to press charges because there wasn't sufficient evidence to show the sexual encounter was non-consensual. It was her word against her perpetrator's.

The sexual assault coupled with the denial of justice sent Maya into a negative spiral. She dropped out of college her freshman year and started making some reckless choices that led to even worse decisions. Within the course of one year, Maya—a straight-A student who had never tasted a drop of alcohol—was swept into a toxic vortex of alcoholism and prescription drug addiction.

Watching his sister's life unravel was more than Jamal could handle. He instinctively wanted to protect Maya, but he didn't know how. Leah wanted to help, too. She was very compassionate toward her sister-in-law, but Leah also knew she and Jamal had limitations with what they could do. The couple had two young children and were struggling to make ends meet financially.

After Jamal's pleading, Leah reluctantly agreed for Maya to live with them following her release from treatment in rehab. Jamal and Maya's father had already died, and their mother was in poor health. As the surviving patriarch of the family, Jamal felt a responsibility to care for his sister, and he also believed home was the only safe place she had.

Maya moved in after 30 days of sobriety. She had a brightness back in her eyes again, and she started helping around the house and exploring college programs so she could return to school. Everything seemed headed in the right direction until she randomly encountered the man who had raped her, which triggered a relapse. When Leah came home with her children that afternoon, Maya was passed out on the couch with a half-empty bottle of whiskey and some prescription pain pills that Leah had kept hidden in the back of the medicine cabinet.

The kids began to cry and scream when they saw their aunt lying unconscious on the couch. At first, Leah thought Maya might actually be dead, so she frantically called 9-1-1. Emergency services arrived in minutes, and the paramedics started working on Maya. After a night in the hospital, it was clear Maya would survive the incident, but Leah was deeply unsettled by the experience.

Jamal and Leah got into the first real conflict of their marriage as they argued about what to do going forward. Jamal insisted that his sister should stay and demanded for Leah to respect him and trust his judgment. In turn, Leah felt disrespected by how the conversation transpired. She had real concerns about the safety of their children and felt strongly that Maya needed to find somewhere else to stay.

In the midst of her frustration, Leah confided in her father. She had always been a "daddy's girl" who could talk to her father about anything, but this conversation was different. In the past, Leah hadn't shared any details about her disagreements with Jamal out of respect for her husband and their marriage. This time, however, the filter was off, and she unleashed a 30–minute tirade about Jamal's sister and everything Jamal had done wrong from first day of their marriage up to the present.

Leah wasn't thinking about the ramifications; she was just hurting and looking for a safe place to vent. She felt helpless over the situation but knew her dad would comfort her, see her point of view, and make her feel better. Leah didn't realize it at the time, but she had inadvertently set in motion a disastrous set of circumstances.

After the call to her dad, Leah drove around for a while to try to clear her head before returning home. As she pulled into her driveway, she was surprised to see her dad's car parked in the yard. As she opened her door, Leah heard voices shouting obscenities at each other from inside the house. She sprinted across the yard and ran to the wide-open front door to see what was happening.

From the doorway Leah saw her dad engaged in a yelling match with her husband. The kids were also present, and they were screaming and crying. Leah positioned herself between the two most significant men in her life. She wanted to intervene in the shouting match before it escalated into a physical fight. Leah pleaded with her dad to leave, and he finally relented, returned to his car, and drove home. As he stomped to his car, her dad was still shouting insults in Jamal's direction and loudly advising Leah to divorce her husband.

After calming the kids and making sure they were settled in their rooms, Leah and Jamal sat down for one of the most important (and most uncomfortable) conversations they'd ever had. There were tears. There were apologies. Eventually, there were solutions.

Leah and Jamal admitted that night that their marriage and home had spiraled out of control because they had lost sight of the priorities God ordained and designed every marriage to uphold.

They agreed that moving forward they would focus on the unity in their marriage and always uphold these priorities:

1. **God**

2. **Their Marriage**

3. **Their Kids**

4. **Their Extended Families and Close Friends**

5. **Everyone Else**

From that point forward, anytime a disagreement threatened the unity of their marriage, Leah and Jamal would revisit their list of priorities to see if they were putting anything in the wrong order. They agreed that they would not bring extended family members into their disagreements as Leah had done with her father. They also promised not to jeopardize their marriage or family again by choosing to help another relative who had problems at a level such as Jamal's sister.

When a couple has their priorities in order, the whole family comes into harmony.

Leah and Jamal committed to work on becoming the best parents they could possibly be. They had been on autopilot, but they now understood that they couldn't use their kids or the busyness of life as an excuse. They wisely recognized that when a couple has their priorities in order, the whole family comes into harmony. If you give your relationship with your kids priority over your spouse, then you will very likely end up with a broken or codependent relationship with your children along with a broken or non-existent relationship with your spouse. Leah and Jamal didn't want to wind up with an empty nest and an empty marriage. They wanted to give their kids the multi-generational blessing of seeing a mom and dad completely committed to God and to their marriage.

The night of the big blow-up, Jamal and Leah stayed up very late talking, laughing, crying, praying, planning, and reprioritizing. At the conversation's end, they had many new and renewed plans and commitments. They'd also decided that the best thing for Maya (and for the health of their family) would be for her to move out. They agreed to continue to help her, but they helped her move into a faith-based group home for women recovering from addiction.

The move proved to be the exact environment Maya needed for the next phase of her recovery. It was also the best thing for Jamal, Leah, and their kids. The solution that is best for one member of the family often proves to be the best for every member of the family. The family often visits "Aunt Maya," and they are helping her make plans for her future while cheering her on every step of the way to full recovery.

Jamal and Leah's dad were eventually able to patch up their relationship too. They both had to swallow some pride, which is a necessary step in resolving almost every conflict, but they put their egos aside and reconciled for the sake of maintaining a healthy relationship. Leah also apologized to both of them for the part she played in setting the stage for their conflict.

Perhaps you can't relate to any of the specific details of Jamal and Leah's story, but every couple can relate to having issues that threaten their marriage's unity. As these issues arise, it's important to address them with honesty and to have compassion for your spouse's point of view. If you keep your priorities in the right order, then you and your spouse will be able to work through anything that comes your way.

One of the most difficult and delicate aspects of in-law relationships comes about when nobody has done anything necessarily "wrong," yet the current dynamic is unsustainable. In these situations, the status quo feels unmanageable, but it also seems impossible to change things without seriously hurting the feelings of the people you love. These situations require a lot of communication, clarity, and compassion.

One such situation involves our friends Ray and Julie. Ray's tech company job transferred him to Austin, Texas, when the company relocated its headquarters. Ray had been working remotely from his hometown, but the company changed its policies and required employees to relocate to keep their jobs. At the time of the move, Austin was the hottest real estate market in the entire country, and house hunting was demoralizing because Ray and Julie couldn't find anything they could afford.

Ray's parents offered to help. They were retiring and said they could relocate to Austin to share a house with Ray and Julie and help take care of their three young kids. Ray was absolutely thrilled at the prospect. On the surface, it seemed like the perfect solution for the multiple issues the family was facing because of the relocation.

Julie loved Ray's parents, and she was genuinely excited to have some help with childcare, but she was also apprehensive about sharing space every day with other people. She was afraid that she would never feel completely at ease in her own home and that she and Ray would never have privacy together. Even so, Julie elected not to voice her concerns. She just kept telling herself that everything would probably work out fine.

The first few months were a transition for everyone, but after some awkward reshuffling around the new house, they all seemed to be settling into a nice groove. Ray's parents were very helpful with the kids, and they also tried to be respectful of Ray and Julie's privacy, at least as much as they could in a crowded house. Ray was happy and satisfied with how well he thought things were working out, and his parents seemed thrilled too.

Naturally, Ray assumed Julie was also happy with the arrangement, especially since she never said anything about her discomfort. Meanwhile, Julie was feeling guilty and selfish because deep down, she wasn't thrilled about sharing the house with Ray's parents. She thought she had disqualified herself from having an opinion because she didn't speak up when they were first discussing the possibility. Julie didn't know how to process her thoughts and feelings, so she quietly built resentment little by little.

Julie found a full-time job outside the home and tried to convince herself that the whole situation with Ray's parents was the best thing for the family. Everyone settled into a routine, and things genuinely seemed to be working out for the whole family until tragedy struck.

Ray's dad contracted COVID–19, and after one week on a ventilator in the ICU, he passed away. He had been a healthy and active man all his life, and the family was shocked when their patriarch was so quickly and cruelly snatched from them. The entire family entered into a season of grief unlike anything any of them had ever experienced.

Around six months after the funeral, the family was settled into a somber routine they all thought of as their "new normal." They were going through the motions, but every aspect of their lives seemed more difficult. They felt as though they were walking through a swamp without waders.

Ray and Julie started drifting apart during this season. Julie was very compassionate about the entire grieving process, and she tried to be supportive and give Ray space to grieve. However, Ray and his mom seemed to be grieving together in a way that made Julie feel excluded. Ray had also become a sort of surrogate spouse to his mom, trying to meet the emotional needs his dad had once filled.

Julie recognized the pain Ray and his mom were experiencing, but she was also beginning to feel cheated. In Julie's mind, Ray now had two wives, and he was giving the best of his time and attention to the one who wasn't Julie. She wondered if she would ever again be the "woman of the house" or have her husband's full attention. Julie felt guilty for her emotions, so she just kept up her silence.

Eventually, Ray's mom told him she needed some time away. She wanted to clear her head and visit some other friends and family members. She had been feeling this way for some time, but she also felt conflicted because the family had come to rely on her for childcare. Ray's mom loved spending time with her grandkids, and she didn't want to put Ray and Julie in a tough situation, so she had also ignored her own feelings and kept up the routine.

Ray encouraged his mom to do whatever she needed to do. He assured her that the family would manage while she was gone. Ray broke the news to Julie, certain that she would be upset because of the loss of his mom's support around the house. Julie immediately burst into tears, and as Ray gently rubbed her back, he said, "I knew this news would be hard for you, but don't worry. We will figure it out." "No," Julie quickly responded, "I'm not crying because I'm upset. I am crying because I'm happy and because I feel guilty for feeling happy. I have wanted you back. I've wanted our family back. I love your mom so much, and I'm so appreciative of all she does for us, but I've secretly hoped she would move out for a long time."

Ray's face couldn't conceal his shock. At first, he took a long pause, and then he asked, "Why didn't you tell me?" Julie saw the bewildered look in his eyes and realized her silence and dutiful-wife act had only prolonged her own pain and perpetuated the distance between her and her husband. Ray also felt guilty because he had completely missed his wife's suffering while he was consumed with his own grief. A painful and honest conversation ensued, but it needed to happen. In fact, it needed to happen for a very long time. There were tears and apologies, followed by forgiveness, reconciliation, breakthrough, and renewed understanding.

Be Honest and Loving in Your Words

Many conversations do not take this positive turn, but everyone involved in Ray and Julie's family loved each other. They all wanted good things for each other, yet they let a fear of potentially difficult conversations perpetuate a stressful situation. Love will overcome but not if we remain silent. Every situation is unique, so there's no one-size-fits-all template for how to have these hard conversations. Still, one universal truth is that the conversations need to happen.

We must share with our spouses the deepest concerns of our hearts and minds and even those concerns that are not so deep. Be honest! Yes, it is important to consider other people's feelings, but you can't constantly hide your own feelings. You must tell the truth. Keeping secrets from your spouse will eventually cause false assumptions and unnecessary stress in your marriage. You might be just one difficult conversation away from a positive breakthrough in your family. Start by sharing what's on your heart. Talk to your spouse about your feelings and concerns. When we speak the truth in love, the truth has the power to set us free.

Love will overcome but not if we remain silent.

Choosing to be an honest spouse is one of the most important choices you will ever make for the health and happiness of your marriage and family. Taking a stand for honesty, even when it costs you something, is a way to honor God, display integrity, and walk in wisdom. Fear may tempt you to be fake in what you say, in what you do, and even in what you post on social media, but you have the power in the Lord to rise above those temptations and choose to be real and honest. God has no greater joy than when He sees His children walking in truth (see 3 John 1:4).

A major theme in the Bible is honesty. Scripture addresses truthfulness in all areas of life. There are Scripture passages about honesty in business, in courtrooms, and in relationships. Here are some thought-provoking verses about honesty:

An honest witness tells the truth;
a false witness tells lies (Proverbs 12:17).

I know, my God, that you test the heart and are pleased with integrity. All these things I have given willingly and with honest intent. And now

I have seen with joy how willingly your people who are here have given to you (1 Chronicles 29:17 NIV).

Dear children, let us not love with words or speech but with actions and in truth (1 John 3:18 NIV).

For the Scriptures say,

"If you want to enjoy life
  and see many happy days,
keep your tongue from speaking evil
  and your lips from telling lies.
Turn away from evil and do good.
  Search for peace, and work to maintain it" (1 Peter 3:10–11).

Do not lie to each other, since you have taken off your old self with its practices (Colossians 3:9 NIV).

If you claim to be religious but don't control your tongue, you are fooling yourself, and your religion is worthless (James 1:26).

Honesty is an expression of love. The honest answer is always the right answer, especially when spoken with love and respect. Since the truth requires love, we must be careful not to speak cruelty cloaked in truth. Honesty is not a license to be everyone's critic. Be an encourager. The world has plenty of critics already. Your family needs your words to be true but let them also be loving, encouraging, and compassionate.

Being loving and kind doesn't mean you'll never have to share a difficult truth with your spouse, a parent, or an in-law. The Bible also tells us that love will sometimes compel us to speak a truth that is hard to say and hard to hear. In those delicate moments, be honest, direct, and kind, but also make sure your intentions are based purely on helping everyone involved rather than being "right." Let love be the motive behind your words. We must also be humble enough to hear honest words of correction spoken to us. Honestly requires humility, both in how we speak and in how we listen.

Choose Your Words and Tone Wisely

Your words have more power than you realize. Every word carries weight, including those you speak to your spouse, children, parents, siblings, and in-laws. Even the words you post on social media have potency. The words you choose to speak and the tone in which you speak them have the power to build people up or tear people down (see Ephesians 4:29). Your tone will shape and influence the tone of your marriage and family.

> Your tone will shape and influence
> the tone of your marriage and family.

Pastor Jimmy Evans, our dear friend and the founder of XO Marriage, has taught many times on the concept of tone in communication. He says you can say the same sentence at least three different ways, and although the words are the same, the tone changes the meaning of the statement entirely. It is important for us to remember that what we say and what others hear us say are two very important parts of communication. All communication embodies an attitude and a spirit. The technical choice and order of words is irrelevant if the tone is wrong. Pastor Jimmy says our tone should communicate *care* and *respect.* Without those elements, you simply cannot communicate effectively. As humans, we hear through our deepest needs.[1] So choose a positive tone. The book of Proverbs reminds us,

> A gentle answer deflects anger,
> but harsh words make tempers flare (Proverbs 15:1).

In Jesus' famous Sermon on the Mount, He gives special praise to "peacemakers" (see Matthew 5:9 NIV) and calls them "children of God. In every situation, we have the unique opportunity to be either peacemakers or instigators. Let your default mode be peace. Be slow to anger and slow to take offense. Don't be the person who tries to stir up drama. Choose to believe the best about people and their motives. Look for common ground. Everywhere you go should be a better place because of the words you speak.

When trying to find common ground and defuse tense situations, your ears are as important as your mouth. The more you listen, the more credibility you'll have when you speak. Pride will tempt you to shout until your point is heard, but the humble path to wisdom will give you the discipline to lean in and listen. You may have a lot you can teach others, but all of us still have plenty to learn. Seek understanding even more than you seek to be understood. Promote healing and unity in your family more than you try to win arguments.

The Bible tells us that the power of life and death is in the tongue (see Proverbs 18:21). Our words have immense power to tear down or build up. God created the entire universe using only the power of His words, and then He created us in His image, giving us power in our words. Use this power for good and not evil. Strive to be a peacemaker.

While our default mode should always be one of peace, there will be times in life when we must speak up and correct others, just like Jesus corrected the nit-picking, drama-raising Pharisees. In these delicate moments, we must be simultaneously humble and bold. Our boldness should be rooted in a desire for the truth, along with the courage to speak it. Our humility comes from a sincere desire for our corrective words to build others up.

If we will allow the Holy Spirit to fill our hearts and guide our steps, then He will give us wisdom with our words in the moments when we might not know what to say or how to say it. If you live surrendered to God, then He will empower you with the wisdom you need in every conversation. Wisdom is not the same as eloquence, so don't feel the need to make your words poetic. Simply speak the truth in love, and you'll be on the right track.

These difficult conversations feel much more productive when every family member involved longs for unity and truly loves one another. Sadly, though, we know this isn't always the case. It can feel like a different scenario entirely when one relative is perpetually divisive and unloving. In the next chapter, we'll explore how to navigate the minefields of a vindictive relative and discuss how to protect your marriage and your sanity in the process.

Avoiding Unnecessary Conversations

We have spent most of this chapter telling you why and how to have difficult conversations, but there are also times when difficult conversations should be avoided. When something is directly impacting your marriage or your life, then you should definitely have a conversation, but in other instances, the act of inserting ourselves into an extended family situation might cause more harm than good. We must learn how to discern when it's best to speak and give advice and when our words might cause more harm than good.

I (Dave) had a Great-Great Aunt Pearl who lived to be 103. When she turned 100, we threw a big birthday party for her, and the local news showed up to do a story about this significant event. The reporter asked Aunt Pearl about her secret to a long life. She thought for a second, laughed out loud, and then said, "I suppose one of the secrets is to mind your own business!"

Aunt Pearl had some wisdom there. Certainly, as followers of Jesus, we are sometimes called to get involved in others' situations, especially when we see someone being bullied, suffering pain, or facing injustice. In those times, we should spring into action to provide whatever help we can. Injustice and suffering are always "our business" when we can help.

However, we live in a time when social media has made it easier than ever to think *everything* is our business and *every* topic is an opportunity for us to take offense, start arguments, and correct everyone whose opinions differ from our own. Wisdom leads us to listen and serve others much more readily than it tells us to correct or confront others. We can't make every issue our top priority. The only time it is right to insert ourselves uninvited into others' situations is when we are ministering rather than meddling. Knowing the difference between those two can be complicated sometimes. Jesus gives us a vivid example of what uninvited ministering looks like in His famous parable of the Good Samaritan (see Luke 10:30–37). In the story, a man was beaten, robbed, and left for dead. Several religious leaders passed by the bloodied victim, but they chose not to get involved. A foreigner from Samaria, with plenty of excuses not to stop, selflessly decided to serve this victim by sacrificing his own time and financial resources.

Jesus hailed this "Good Samaritan" as the quintessential example of what it means to be a good neighbor and show love for others. When given the opportunity to serve selflessly, we should always do it. When we see someone in desperate need and it is within our power to help, we must pray, put our faith into action, and help!

The difference between the example of the Good Samaritan and inserting yourself into someone else's affairs in a negative way comes down largely to your own motives. When you're motivated by selfish pride, you'll find yourself feeling entitled to correct others. When you're motivated by love, you'll find yourself feeling compelled to serve others. Love brings healing and unity, but pride brings destruction and division.

Don't let argumentative relatives bait you into senseless conflicts and arguments. Be kind even to unkind people. Your kindness is not a reflection of their character. It reflects God's character. He is loving and patient with us even at our worst moments. Strive to be a peacemaker in your family. As ambassadors of Christ on earth, make it your mission to be like Him in all situations (see 2 Corinthians 5:18–19).

Love brings healing and unity, but pride brings destruction and division.

By His example, Jesus showed us when to intervene and when to stay out of an argument. He helped all those in His path who needed His help and lovingly taught all those who came to Him with a desire to learn. But Jesus never fell into the trap of wasting His time and energy debating with people who only wanted to argue. When people tried to trap Him in no-win situations, Jesus showed love and spoke the truth, but He also had the wisdom and restraint to walk away.

When you know someone in your family needs your help, follow Jesus' example and offer help. And when you experience someone goading you into a divisive argument, let wisdom lead you to walk away. Even if you're sitting at the same Thanksgiving table with family, you don't have to engage in every political argument or divisive disagreement. When you're not sure whether a complicated situation requires your intervention or your absence, ask the Holy Spirit to guide you.

When you allow God to shepherd your heart with His Spirit and His principles, He will give you the discernment you need in difficult moments. Do your best to live at peace with all people, especially your family, but recognize that some people will refuse to live at peace with you. When that happens, pray for them and love them from a distance. Don't sink to the level of those who want to sling mud. Always take the high road as you protect the unity in your marriage.

Study Guide

for Individuals and Groups

Group leaders should prepare prior to the group meeting with the following steps:

- *Review Chapter 6.*

- *Read 1 Chronicles 29:17; Proverbs 12:17; 15:1; 18:21; and Matthew 5:9.*

- *Choose one discussion question and one reflection question for group engagement in case time runs short.*

- *Pray for each group member by name. Ask the Lord to prepare their hearts and minds.*

- *If possible, silence your cell phone and remove any other distractions. Be fully present for your group and prepare to see lives transformed by God.*

Chapter 6 Summary

God ordained and designed every marriage to uphold unity and these priorities in this order:

1. God

2. Their Marriage

3. Their Kids

4. Their Extended Families and Close Friends

5. Everyone Else

When a couple has their priorities in order, the whole family comes into harmony. As issues arise, it is important to address them with honesty and have compassion for your spouse's point of view. If you keep your priorities in the right order, then you and your spouse will be able to work through anything that comes your way.

Love will overcome but not if we remain silent. We must share with our spouse the deepest concerns of our hearts and minds. Be honest! It is important to consider other people's feelings, but you must tell the truth. Keeping secrets from your spouse will eventually cause false assumptions and unnecessary stress in your marriage. You might be just one difficult conversation away from a positive breakthrough in your family. Start by sharing what is on your heart. Talk to your spouse about your feelings and concerns. When we speak the truth in love, the truth has the power to set us free.

Your words have more power than you realize. Your tone will shape and influence the tone of your marriage and family. Pastor Jimmy Evans says our tone should communicate *care* and *respect.* Without those elements, you simply cannot communicate effectively.

The Bible tells us that the power of life and death is in the tongue (see Proverbs 18:21). We must be simultaneously humble and bold. Our boldness should be rooted in a desire for the truth, along with the courage to speak it. Our humility comes from a sincere desire for our corrective words to build others up. If we will allow the Holy Spirit to fill our hearts and guide our steps, then He will give us wisdom with our words in these moments when we might not know what to say or how to say it. If you live surrendered to God, then He will empower you with the wisdom you need in every conversation.

Wisdom leads us to listen and serve others much more readily than it tells us to correct or confront others. The only times it is right to insert ourselves uninvited into others' situations is when we are ministering rather than meddling. Do your best to live at peace with all people, especially your family, but recognize that some people will refuse to live at peace with you. When that happens, pray for them and love them from a distance.

Discussion

1. As you read the list of priorities, when was a time you got them in the wrong order? What happened as a result?

2. How is it possible to be honest and loving at the same time?

3. What are some examples of times when we should keep silent?

Reflection

1. How does someone's tone influence how you hear what they are saying? How does your tone influence others?

2. How has the Holy Spirit guided you in your words as you talk with your spouse?

3. What steps can you take to communicate with your family more effectively?

4. Have you ever found it impossible to live at peace with someone? How did you deal with the situation? Would you deal with it differently today?

Prayer

Father God, I want my words to have the right effect. Please guard my heart and guide my tongue as I speak to my spouse and other family members. I confess I have not always used my words to build up others. Please forgive me and help me make those situations right. Teach me to be silent when I should. I want to be at peace with everyone. I trust Your Holy Spirit to give me wisdom so I can improve in this area of my life. I always want to use my words to honor You and give You praise for the good things You have done. In Jesus' name, Amen.

SECTION THREE

SPECIAL CASES

And do everything with love.

—1 Corinthians 16:14

My husband and I are temporarily living with his parents after falling on some diffi-cult financial circumstances. I love my in-laws, but the financial strain we're facing combined with the lack of privacy is really causing tension in the house. I feel stuck. We also have a special needs son who is only two years old. My mother-in-law helps with him while my husband and I go to work. I'm very thankful for my in-laws and their hospitality, but this whole situation feels unsustainable. I feel like I'm creating a debt with them that I can never repay. They not-so-subtly drop little comments often about how much they're doing for us. I wish we could move out, but we can't afford anything right now, and I could never find specialized childcare for my son until he gets older. I feel like this whole situation is a powder keg ready to blow. I feel guilty for resenting my in-laws when they're doing so much for us, and I feel like they probably resent the situation as much as I do. I want a healthy relationship with everyone in this house, but the longer we stay, the more damage I feel like we're all doing to each other.

—Madison L. (Married 3 years)

Aging Parents, Living with Family, and Estrangement

When Your In-Law Is Widowed or Divorced

Years ago, our dear friend Zara called us with great news: she had met someone incredibly special and was engaged to be married. We were thrilled for her! As Zara told us about her future husband, Jeremy, we could almost see her smiling through the phone. She told us how kind he was and how much he loved the Lord. Zara said he challenged her to grow deeper in her relationship with Jesus. She simply adored Jeremy, and we could feel how excited she was to marry him.

When we asked about Jeremy's family, Zara paused. Then, with a sigh, she told us that she truly loved Jeremy's mom and that she was very kind. Even so, Zara was concerned that Jeremy's mom was going to have a tough time when the couple transitioned into marriage. Jeremy's dad passed away when he was a teenager, and ever since, the mother looked to Jeremy to fulfill the void left by his father. When Jeremy was single, he was able to tend to his mother's need for attention, errands, and other tasks. However, now that he was engaged and soon to be married to Zara, his priorities were starting to change, and his mother didn't like these changes at all.

As the couple neared their wedding date, Jeremy's mother seemed to grow more frustrated each day. This growing attitude became very concerning to Jeremy and Zara, and he felt as if he was being pulled in two. He deeply loved his mother and wanted to be a "good" son, but he also deeply loved Zara and wanted to be a "good" husband. As believers, Zara and Jeremy wanted to live out a biblical marriage, and they knew this would require setting healthy boundaries with his mother. They also knew it would be a very delicate process.

During the days and months leading up to the wedding, Zara and Jeremy discussed what boundaries they should establish for their marriage to thrive *and* for his mother to have her needs met as a widow. They decided to have a discussion with his mother and pick one day a week when she and he, sometimes along with Zara, would spend time together, run errands, or do anything else to meet his mom's needs. This plan would be a practical, loving way to serve Jeremy's mom while also maintaining autonomy over the majority of their schedules. Jeremy would also frequently remind his mom that she wasn't *losing* a son, as she would often say; rather, she was *gaining* a sweet daughter-in-law. Zara made great efforts to show Jeremy's mother kindness. Zara invited her to do some fun things together, such as going out for lunch, shopping, or getting pedicures. Both Zara and Jeremy tried to honor his mother and allay her fears while also creating the healthy boundaries they needed to prioritize their own marriage. It took lots of prayer, frequent check-ins with one another and with his mother, and loads of grace from everyone.

When we revisited the situation with Zara and Jeremy years later, they reported some bumpy times with his mom, but they committed to praying, talking, checking in, holding tightly to their boundaries, and monitoring and adjusting as necessary. It took a lot of grace, but Jeremy and Zara have been married over a decade now, and they have a wonderful relationship with his mother and with Zara's parents.

When parents or in-laws are single from either death or divorce, everyone experiences a wide range of emotions. It can be complicated, and feelings can be hurt so easily. Therefore, it is important to talk openly and honestly with your spouse about your own feelings, concerns, and expectations as you navigate these relationships. We must resist the urge to point fingers and assume the worst of our spouse or in-laws. This doesn't mean we ignore the real problems that are in front of us; rather, we should keep a soft heart and an open, positive mindset. This attitude is rarely easy, but when we choose to lean on God and trust that He is working all things together for our good and His glory, we can do this (see Romans 8:28).

> We must resist the urge to point fingers and assume the worst of our spouse or in-laws.

Let's return to the story of Ruth and Naomi, which we discussed in Chapter 1. Naomi was Ruth's *former* mother-in-law, but the two women felt a deep loyalty to one another and maintained something closer to a mother-daughter relationship. Ruth was a Moabite. For many years, the Israelites had avoided or even frowned upon her people. Still, she followed Naomi back to Bethlehem instead of going back to her own family in Moab (see Ruth 1:16–18). The Bible does not reveal why Ruth made this decision. We only know that Naomi encouraged Ruth to return to her family multiple times. When Naomi made the same plea to her other former daughter-in-law, Orpah, she did go home to her family. The Bible records Ruth's response this way: "When Naomi realized that Ruth was determined to go with her, she stopped urging her" (Ruth 1:18 NIV).

We may not know exactly what Ruth was thinking when she went with Naomi, but the Scriptures do tell us a lot about Naomi's state of mind. Naomi was reeling from the tremendous trauma of losing her husband and two sons. Her pain was unimaginable, and she probably just wanted to be alone. Even so, she was vocal about her agony to those around her, and she even went so far as to change her name to *Mara*, which means 'bitter' (see Ruth 1:20).

When Ruth met and married Boaz, a man from the same tribe as Naomi's deceased husband, Ruth was able to bring Naomi into the familial fold, which guaranteed her ongoing care. I (Ashley) can only imagine what Boaz might have been thinking. That is a lot to take on! However, Boaz showed both women tremendous kindness, and as a couple, Boaz and Ruth showed Naomi honor, love, and respect. Soon after the couple married, Ruth became pregnant and gave birth to a son. In some Bible translations, this part of the story is titled, "Naomi Gains a Son." Isn't that beautiful? I love how the book of Ruth describes the reaction of the townswomen:

> Then the women of the town said to Naomi, "Praise the LORD, who has now provided a redeemer for your family! May this child be famous in Israel. May he restore your youth and care for you in your old age. For he is the son of your daughter-in-law who loves you and has been better to you than seven sons!"
>
> Naomi took the baby and cuddled him to her breast. And she cared for him as if he were her own. The neighbor women said, "Now at last Naomi has a son again!" And they named him Obed. He became the father of Jesse and the grandfather of David (Ruth 4:14–17).

The account of Ruth and Naomi serves as a beautiful reminder of how God can bring peace and unexpected blessings into the midst of complicated situations when we fully surrender to Him and choose to show kindness, honor, patience, grace, respect, and love.

Understanding Our Caretaking Roles

There is a beautiful moment that occurred just before Jesus took His last breath on the cross. He had been deserted by all but a handful of close followers. Among the few remaining to grieve Him were His mother, Mary, and John, His disciple. In Jesus' time, the eldest son had the responsibility to provide care for his widowed or aging mother. Mary was already a widow by this point in the story. She stood helplessly watching not only her Savior but also her oldest son die. With Jesus' death, she was facing both unimaginable grief and great uncertainty about her own financial and physical security.

Jesus looked lovingly and tenderly at His mom. He was giving His life to save her soul, but He wasn't only concerned about her spiritual needs. He also wanted to make sure her physical needs were met. He used some of His final words from the cross to make sure His mother would be cared for:

> When Jesus saw his mother standing there beside the disciple he loved, he said to her, "Dear woman, here is your son." And he said to this disciple, "Here is your mother." And from then on this disciple took her into his home (John 19:26–27).

John wholeheartedly embraced the physical, emotional, and financial burden of bringing another person into his family. He did it joyfully as an extension of his love for Jesus. John chose to love Mary as his own mother because he knew it was God's desire. I'm sure he grew to love Mary, but his initial commitment to her wasn't based on his love and affection for her—it was based on his love and affection for Christ.

This beautiful scene from Scripture gives us so much insight into in-law relationships. We are reminded that showing love for someone isn't dependent on our feelings for that person. Rather, we can show love to a person as an extension of our love for God and as a loving act of obedience, knowing that loving this person is the right thing to do.

C. S. Lewis, one of our favorite Christian authors, had a similar experience in his own life. Decades before he wrote *The Chronicles of Narnia*, he fought alongside his best friend in the British army during World War I. Both men were young and single during the war, so they made a pledge to one another. They promised that if either of them died in battle, then the other would look after his dead friend's mother.

Lewis's friend eventually died in battle. After the war, true to his word, Lewis brought his friend's mother into his own home and cared for her the rest of her life. In this situation, Lewis and his newly adopted mother never fully connected. It was a great sacrifice for Lewis both emotionally and financially to care for this woman, but his trust in God and his love for his friend gave him the strength to remain faithful to his promise. Lewis later wrote that this difficult relationship was a tool God used to refine his own character and help him confront selfishness in his own life.

We would like to think that Jesus's mother, Mary, was a much kinder and sweeter houseguest than C. S. Lewis described in his situation. Regardless, though, the principle stays the same. God blesses our faithfulness when we embrace our commitment to family, even when that "family" isn't necessarily a blood relative.

Love in its purest form is shown in an unwavering commitment to someone who can't repay us. In our examples, both John the disciple and C. S. Lewis showed love by giving their unwavering commitment to another person's mother. They did it based on a sense of duty and their love for the one who asked them to do it. When it comes to our own in-law relationships, we can learn much from their examples.

> Love in its purest form is shown in an unwavering commitment to someone who can't repay us.

The Bible has a lot to say about the importance of caring for family members, but in different times and circumstances, our roles in caring for family members can vary. Relationship dynamics seem to be the most complicated when we are temporarily or permanently living with family members or in-laws. Due to various circumstances, such as finances, health, or childcare, many families chose to share a common home with their parents or in-laws for a season. When considering this kind of living arrangement, it's important to talk through the following questions with your spouse:

1. Is there enough space for all of us to live comfortably? If not, what can we do to make it more comfortable for everyone? Should the kids share a room? Should we try to divide the house or apartment in a way that provides two separate, fully functioning home spaces?

2. What are some concerns about this potential joint living situation? Is it going to burden anyone financially? If so, how can we divide the expenses and responsibilities to make sure all parties are carrying the load?

3. What are some healthy boundaries we need to have in place to protect our marriage and family relationships? Do we need to create a schedule that everyone can agree upon on when it comes to occupying certain spaces in the home, such as a morning or nighttime shower, a bathroom schedule, when company can come over, when kids' playdates will take place, or how far in advance something needs to be scheduled at the home?

These are some of the questions that will help you, your spouse, and your family members or in-laws to think through whether it might be wise or even feasible to share a home. Exploring the questions will help you prepare for the transition if you decide to combine households. You may also want to talk to your family members or in-laws about having a weekly check-in to clear the air and hear each other's concerns. It may also be wise to put a time limit on how long you all plan on sharing a home. For example, you may all agree that you are going to try this arrangement for three months and then reevaluate the situation once the time arrives. This preemptive plan will help everyone involved not to feel overwhelmed by this living situation so they can manage one stint at a time.

If you are moving into your family's home, go out of your way to be conscientious and helpful. Don't disregard their wishes when it comes to their standard of cleanliness, order, or anything else related to the management of the home. If cleaning isn't your forte, then be willing to hire or contribute to a housekeeper. Offer to help with meals whenever you can. As we have worked with families who share a home, the ones who seem to fare the best always mention serving one another and being willing to pitch in and help however they can. An attitude of servanthood goes a long way toward keeping a peaceful, healthy relationship. Don't allow resentment to gain a foothold because one person or couple is pulling more weight while another is slacking off. Agree upfront that you will be gracious and helpful.

If your family or in-laws are moving in with you, then work to preserve their dignity, privacy, and individuality. Do your best to make them feel at home. Many times, parents are almost forced to move into an adult child's home due to health or financial challenges, and they feel as though they are losing some of their autonomy and worth. As their adult children, do your best to support their autonomy by asking if they can do certain tasks. Honor and thank them for the help they give. Their contributions could include cooking, cleaning, fixing things, reading to the kids at night, watching the kids, or running errands. Have clear communication and explicit agreements about what they are willing to do. Ask but don't demand. On the other hand, remember they have their own lives to live. Encourage them to get together with friends, become involved in church and the community, and invite their friends into the home. Include them in family activities, but don't assume they should always participate. It is appropriate for you, your spouse, and your children to want to do some things on your own, so don't feel guilty about that. Make sure your family member understands that you are not excluding them. The main thing to remember is not to take advantage of one another or make assumptions without conversations. Keep your hearts soft towards each other, assume the best, and if you have any concerns, then bring them up and talk about them sooner rather than later.

Also, it is wise to create a space in your home where you can be alone to pray or enjoy some personal space. In turn, be willing to help your loved one have their personal space as well. We all need a place to retreat—especially those of us who are introverts. It's a balance that requires a lot of prayer, communication, grace, monitoring, and adjusting, but sharing a home can be done well when you follow these suggestions.

Estrangement

One of the hardest in-law situations to cope with is estrangement, which is similar to the ghost in-law dynamic we discussed earlier. When your family or in-laws decide to vanish from your life, it is heartbreaking. You and your spouse might have been the ones who chose to put some distance in place for a time, or maybe your family or in-laws stopped answering your calls and texts. Maybe you insisted that certain boundaries be in place, and your family or in-laws didn't want to abide by those guidelines. Sometimes, family members or in-laws can fall on hard times due to financial setbacks or addictions, so they avoid their family members out of shame. Whatever the reason for an estrangement, we must keep on praying and believing that God will bring restoration to our relationships, even if it takes a lifetime.

We can keep our hearts soft towards our loved ones by praying for them. It is really hard to keep hating someone while praying for them at the same time. If you don't believe us, then we encourage you to try it. Prayer is our lifeline, especially in heartbreaking circumstances like estrangement. You may be reading this and thinking, *I've prayed for them every day. I've reached out, only to be ghosted again and again. And my loved one has never taken responsibility or sought forgiveness for the hurt they've caused me!* We understand. It's really hard to keep holding onto hope and trying to be "the bigger person," but one of the most healing and wise things you can do is offer forgiveness even when there's been no apology. We forgive because God first forgave us—before we offered any sort of apology of our own. We can only *give* forgiveness, and it leads to our freedom. It doesn't necessarily mean we let the person who wronged us off the hook, but it does mean that we are believing God to deal with their heart accordingly. Trust, however, is a different thing. It cannot be given; it can only be earned. Once we forgive, we give the person who wronged us the chance to earn back our trust by their consistent actions. We can love and forgive someone without trusting them. It is not ideal, but it's possible.

> One of the most healing and wise things you can do is offer forgiveness even when there's been no apology.

Don't lose hope if your family members or in-laws are estranged from you. Ask God to move in your situation and keep reaching out to your estranged loved ones from time to time. Send them a card on their birthday, even if you know one won't be coming your way on yours. If you run into them, smile and say hello. If they do not respond, then it's okay to grieve that moment and allow yourself time to process those emotions. However, do not let bitterness, hopelessness, or resentment take root. Keep praying and believing that God is working in your situation. He is with you.

CHAPTER 7

Study Guide

for Individuals and Groups

Group leaders should prepare prior to the group meeting with the following steps:

- *Review Chapter 7.*

- *Read John 19:26–27 and Romans 8:28.*

- *Choose one discussion question and one reflection question for group engagement in case time runs short.*

- *Pray for each group member by name. Ask the Lord to prepare their hearts and minds.*

- *If possible, silence your cell phone and remove any other distractions. Be fully present for your group and prepare to see lives transformed by God.*

Chapter 7 Summary

When parents or in-laws are single from either death or divorce, everyone experiences a wide range of emotions. It can be complicated, and feelings can be hurt so easily. Therefore, it is important to talk openly and honestly with your spouse about your own feelings, concerns, and expectations as you navigate these relationships. We must resist the urge to point fingers and assume the worst of our spouse and in-laws. This doesn't mean we should ignore the real problems that are in front of us; rather, it means we should keep a soft heart and an open, positive mindset. God can bring peace and unexpected blessings into the midst of complicated situations when we fully surrender to Him and choose to show kindness, honor, patience, grace, respect, and love.

Showing love for someone is not dependent on our feelings for that person. It is an extension of our love for God. He blesses our faithfulness when we embrace our commitment to family, even when that "family" isn't necessarily a blood relative. Love in its purest form is shown in an unwavering commitment to someone who can't repay us.

Relationship dynamics seem to be the most complicated when we are temporarily or permanently living with family members or in-laws. When considering this kind of living arrangement, it is important to talk it through with your spouse. Exploring the questions we raise in this chapter will help you prepare for the transition if you decide to combine households.

One of the hardest in-law situations to cope with is estrangement. When family members or in-laws decide to vanish from your life, it is heartbreaking, but we can keep our hearts soft towards our loved ones by praying for them. It's really hard to keep holding onto hope and trying to be "the bigger person," but one of the most healing and wise things you can do is offer forgiveness even when there's been no apology. Keep praying and believing that God is working in your situation. He is with you.

Discussion

1. Has a family member experienced a death or divorce that has affected your marriage? Explain what happened.

2. Have you ever tried to live with a family member or have one live with you and your spouse? What was that experience like?

3. How would you advise someone who is planning on living in the same house with other family members?

Reflection

1. How can we deal with estrangement when it happens in our relationships? What is God's plan for those situations?

2. Do you have someone you need to forgive even though they have not offered an apology?

3. Have you and your spouse discussed how to help widowed or divorced parents? If not, is this a conversation you should have?

Prayer

Father God, I want to honor my family members and in-laws. Please teach my spouse and me how we can show honor while keeping You and our marriage as our top priorities. I know I have often wanted to hold on to anger and resentment when You tell me to forgive. Work in my heart this very moment. I want my heart to be tender toward You and others. Help me as I choose to reconcile with our family members. Thank You for loving me and bringing me peace. Help me to show Your love and peace to others. In Jesus' name, Amen.

CHAPTER 8

Religious and Familial Differences

Religious Differences

There is a hero in the Bible whose story you may have never heard before. His name is Jethro, and his relationship with his son-in-law Moses had a world-changing impact. Jethro's positive influence as a supportive father-in-law is a practical and inspirational example for us to follow. In Exodus chapter 18, we learn that Moses and Jethro came from vastly different cultural and religious backgrounds, but they forged a very healthy relationship. There's so much we can learn from the relational dynamic between these two men.

As a quick refresher, Moses was born in ancient Egypt during a time when the Hebrew people were enslaved. Being born a slave is a terrible way to start out life, but to make matters even worse, the Pharaoh (Egypt's leader) felt threatened by the growing Hebrew population, so he ordered the murder of all male Jewish babies at the time of their birth.

Moses's mother was terrified as she held her crying baby boy. She knew the soldiers would come for him, so she made the desperate decision to create a waterproof basket and send her baby floating down the Nile River with her older daughter following from the shore to make sure Moses arrived somewhere safe. The baby finally landed near the Pharaoh's palace, and by God's perfect plan, Pharaoh's own daughter plucked the infant out of the river and decided to adopt him.

Moses grew up as a prince of Egypt. His adoptive royal mother made sure he had the best of everything. He lived in luxury and power while his people remained enslaved and abused. When Moses grew to adulthood and became fully aware of his own past, he decided to reject his adoptive family and do his part to support the Hebrews. He grew frustrated as he was unsure of how to help his people, and in a misguided moment of rage, he killed an Egyptian soldier who was abusing a Hebrew slave.

As a murderer who felt estranged from both his birth and adoptive families, Moses fled to the desert. His life had no direction—he did not know how to move forward, and he definitely could not go back. This future leader of one of the world's most significant movements found himself at rock bottom. Moses was now a fugitive with no power, no family, no possessions, and no prospects for the future.

During his time on the run, Moses connected with a nomadic tribe led by a man named Jethro. In a world very skeptical of foreigners, Jethro decided to welcome Moses into his family and treat him with love and respect. Moses eventually married Jethro's daughter Zipporah and started a family of his own.

The Bible does not provide every detail of Moses's decades in the desert far away from Egypt, but we do know that God used that time to prepare Moses for the most important assignment of his life: returning to Egypt to free the Hebrew people from slavery and leading the newly-formed nation of Israel out to the Promised Land. Before Moses left the desert for Egypt, he consulted Jethro, who gave his blessing—"Go in peace" (Exodus 4:18).

Moses did as the Lord instructed him to do, and word soon reached Jethro "about everything God has done for Moses and his people, the Israelites … about how the LORD had rescued them from Egypt" (Exodus 18:1). Jethro came to visit his son–in-law in the wilderness, and it was a much-needed time of reconnection and encouragement.

Moses told his father-in-law everything the LORD had done to Pharaoh and Egypt on behalf of Israel. He also told about all the hardships they had experienced along the way and how the LORD had rescued his people from all their troubles. Jethro was delighted when he heard about all the good things the LORD had done for Israel as he rescued them from the hand of the Egyptians.

"Praise the LORD," Jethro said, "for he has rescued you from the Egyptians and from Pharaoh. Yes, he has rescued Israel from the powerful hand of Egypt! I know now that the LORD is greater than all other gods, because he rescued his people from the oppression of the proud Egyptians."

Then Jethro, Moses' father-in-law, brought a burnt offering and sacrifices to God. Aaron and all the elders of Israel came out and joined him in a sacrificial meal in God's presence (Exodus 18:8–12).

The next day, Jethro got to see Moses's leadership in action, and he quickly realized that Moses was overwhelmed by the massive weight of responsibility. Jethro told Moses, "You're going to wear yourself out—and the people, too. This job is too heavy a burden for you to handle all by yourself" (Exodus 18:18). Jethro encouraged Moses to develop a plan and begin delegating authority. He said, "Let the leaders decide the smaller matters themselves. They will help you carry the load, making the task easier for you. If you follow this advice, and if God commands you to do so, then you will be able to endure the pressures, and all these people will go home in peace" (Exodus 18:22–23).

Other men might have rejected this advice and declared, "God chose *me*, so I am going to handle this all by myself!" But Moses wasn't so prideful or foolish. Instead, he "listened to his father-in-law's advice and followed his suggestions" (v. 24). This humility, coupled with Jethro's wisdom, allowed Moses to develop a healthier, more sustainable system of governance for the people of Israel.

Moses wholeheartedly trusted Jethro's counsel because he had respect for his father-in-law and also because he knew Jethro had no secret agenda. These two men truly were gifts to each other. We believe they modeled God's ultimate plan for in-law relationships. When our relationships are rooted in acceptance and mutual respect, we too can have multigenerational family health that becomes a gift to everyone.

> When our relationships are rooted in acceptance and mutual respect, we too can have multigenerational family health that becomes a gift to everyone.

Acceptance and mutual respect may present some difficulties when families have hugely different religious beliefs. Luciana and Joseph know this all too well. Luciana met Joseph during a Peace Corps assignment. They shared a common heart for helping the under-resourced, so they hit it off right away. As they served together, they also fell in love. They couldn't wait to get back to the US to introduce each other to their families.

Talking openly about their individual families and cultural backgrounds, Joseph and Luciana quickly realized they had a lot of differences. Joseph was raised in a devout Jewish family, and Luciana's family were committed Catholics (although in recent years, Luciana had started attending a non-denominational Christian church). Even with these significant differences, the couple believed that God had brought them together and that love would conquer all. So on the last night of their Peace Corps assignment, Joseph got down on one knee and proposed with a ring made by the locals whom they had served and befriended during their time of service. Luciana cried with joy and gave Joseph an immediate "Yes!" They couldn't wait to get home and share the good news with their parents. Instead of texting their families or making video calls, they decided to make it a surprise. When they got home, they would reveal their plan. The couple believed that once their parents witnessed the deep love they had for each other in person, they would have no reservations about the couple forging a life together. Joseph and Luciana never saw what was coming.

When their families gathered to meet them at the airport state-side, Joseph and Luciana walked out into the airport terminal hand in hand, excited and ready to introduce each other to their families. The minute their families spotted them, the couple could see their parents' eager smiles slowly deflate. Once in their presence, both families fell strangely silent. Neither set of parent would have put the two of them together. They couldn't fathom what they would have in common, and Joseph's family couldn't help but notice the beautiful cross around Luciana's neck.

Luciana squeezed Joseph's hand as if she could relieve some of the obvious tension everyone was feeling at that moment. Joseph nervously broke the silence and said, "Hey, Mom and Dad, it's so good to see you. I want you to meet someone very special to me. This is Luciana ... my fiancée." Joseph's parents' eyes widened as they let this news settle in. Luciana reached out to Joseph's dad, and he reluctantly shook her hand. Luciana did the same with Joseph's mom, who tried to force a smile. When Luciana introduced Joseph to her parents, they greeted him with an embrace. "I guess we should hug since we are going to be family," exclaimed Luciana's mom. Her parents were more expressive in their affection, but their faces still betrayed their concern and reluctance. Things were certainly not off to a good start.

After Luciana and Joseph parted to go to their parents' respective homes, each set of parents began to voice concerns about the couple's plans. Joseph's family had always wanted him to marry a "nice Jewish girl." Sure, he had dated many non-Jewish young women through the years, but his parents always thought he would choose to honor them by settling down with someone who shared their faith. They didn't know that Luciana had introduced Joseph to Jesus during their time in the Peace Corps.

Talking about her faith wasn't something that Luciana forced on Joseph at all. In fact, when Joseph first saw Luciana, she was serving water to some children in need. Joseph was struck by the joy and care that radiated from Luciana. He knew he had to introduce himself to her. So Joseph went up to her and said, "You know, it's almost like you are glowing when you give each child some water. I can tell you really love helping them." Luciana flashed a coy smile, looked at the kids and then back at Joseph, and said, "I do. I really love being here with them. I just wish I could tell them about Who really gives me this glow." At first, Joseph was not sure what she was talking about or if she might be joking, so he asked, "What do you mean? You are glowing because you have a good heart, and frankly it's really hot and sweaty out here with this beaming sun. That is all it is." Luciana smiled and said, "Well, there is some truth to what you are saying. It's blazing out here, but I'm talking about something deeper. You see, I am a Christian. I'm talking about Jesus. I just feel like if these kids knew how much Jesus loved them and had a plan for their lives, they would have more hope than just getting water each day. Still, I will respect the rules of the Peace Corps and not discuss my religious convictions with the people we serve. I am happy to be doing what we are doing to help these amazing people." Joseph was intrigued.

Growing up and attending synagogue, Joseph had learned about God and what He had done for Israel, but he had never really heard the story of Jesus, much less that Jesus might have a plan for Joseph's life. Joseph just knew Jews did not believe that Jesus was the Messiah. They were still waiting for the Messiah and working hard to earn God's forgiveness and favor in the process. Even though Joseph had been a devout Jew from a very early age, he had never really felt whole or that God really loved him in the way that Luciana described.

In the days, weeks, and months that followed, Joseph continued to ask Luciana about her faith, and she told him all about Jesus. Eventually, Joseph accepted Jesus as his Lord and Savior, and Luciana, along with a pastor at a local church, baptized him in the ocean nearby. The experience was so special, and it brought both of them closer to God and each other. Joseph knew his parents would probably take issue with his newfound faith in Christ, but he believed they would accept it over time. He even thought that in the long run he might be able to lead them to Jesus just as

Luciana had done with him. Joseph wanted his parents to experience the love and freedom he now had in Christ. He realized this might be a long shot, but he also knew that with God, all things are possible. Even so, Joseph didn't want to completely disrupt his family. He loved and honored his parents, and he respected his Jewish roots too.

When Joseph's parents expressed how surprised they were that he would want to marry a Christian, he calmly told them that Luciana's pure faith in Jesus is what first drew him to her. He told them about how he accepted Christ and felt freedom and purpose for the first time in his life. Joseph's parents patiently listened until he was finished talking, and then tears welled up in his mother's eyes. She felt betrayed by her son, and she blamed Luciana for it. Joseph's father grew angrier with each word his son shared, and what started as a calm conversation quickly boiled over into a shouting match. His parents told him they would never accept Luciana into their family, and they certainly would not attend the wedding. Joseph was hurt and angry, and he felt like the conversation had reached a dead end. When his dad started saying hateful things about Luciana and her family, he couldn't take it anymore. Joseph stormed off and left the house to go for a drive.

Joseph called Luciana and told her about his family's response. She was very disappointed and upset to hear that they didn't accept Joseph's conversion or their engagement, but she also felt a peace that surpassed understanding in knowing that God was still with them and would work all things together for their good and His glory (see Romans 8:28). The couple prayed together, and each decided they would do their best to love and respect their families, even though their parents opposed their engagement and upcoming marriage. Out of respect for their parents, Joseph and Luciana agreed to postpone their wedding date for a short time. They really wanted their parents to be at the wedding, and they wanted to do their part to be peacemakers, as they had read in Romans 12:18.

During those months of planning their wedding, Joseph and Luciana spent time with each of their families as a couple. Luciana would even invite Joseph's mother out to lunch. Joseph's mom didn't accept the invitation at first, because she saw the acceptance as an endorsement of Joseph and Luciana's relationship. Joseph talked to his mom about this issue, and he asked her to please give Luciana a chance. He told her, "Mom, I know you love me. If you love me, and you know that I love her, then don't you think you could try to love her out of your love for me?" His mom paused for a moment to think. She did love her son so very much, and she wanted to have a good relationship with him and his future wife. Joseph's mom had been so hurt over him falling for someone outside of their faith, and in her eyes, he made matters even worse by deciding to share Luciana's faith as well. Even so, his mom didn't want to lose him. She and Joseph's father went to the synagogue to pray and seek guidance from their rabbi. When they came back home after that meeting, they experienced a shift in their perspective. Joseph's parents called and invited the couple to dinner the following week. Joseph and Luciana accepted the invitation.

At the dinner, Joseph's parents looked genuinely happy to see the couple as they sat down at the table. After some pleasantries, his parents apologized to Luciana, who graciously accepted. They explained that although they had always expected Joseph to follow in their footsteps by keeping the Jewish faith and marrying a Jewish woman, they knew that God had a different plan for him. They told Luciana that they could see a huge difference in Joseph since he came home from the Peace Corps. He was at peace and happy, and he was excited about the future. That was all they ever dreamed about for their son. The parents also commended Luciana on what a kind woman she is, and they even said they were glad that Joseph found someone so kind with whom to share his life. Tears filled Luciana's eyes as they said these things, and she looked at Joseph with awe and relief.

Months after that pivotal dinner, the couple married in a non-denominational church where they had connected with other believers through pre-marital classes. Both families were there, and everyone was beaming with joy. God had done a miracle in Joseph and Luciana's eyes. They knew things might get a little bumpy in the future with the two of them coming from different backgrounds, but they also knew that they could get through anything that came their way as long as they remained united and continued to trust in God's help.

If you and your spouse come from different religious backgrounds and your family or in-laws are opposed to your union, then do your best to resist the urge to see them as enemies. Instead, follow Joseph and Luciana's example and be patient. Show respect for your families' concerns and love them through it. Be prepared for awkward moments and even disagreements, but don't let negative comments bring out the worst in you. Stand your ground kindly but firmly. Remind your family members that your spouse is the one you have chosen to share your life with, and you would love it if they could try to love the person you chose as well.

Remind your family members that your spouse is the one you have chosen to share your life with, and you would love it if they could try to love the person you chose as well.

If your family chooses not to love your spouse and instead engages in derogatory insults or shows disrespect toward your spouse, then you must address the situation. The least your family member can do is maintain civility and keep negative comments to themselves. This difficult conversation is easier said than done, but the more you stick to your boundaries and stand up for your spouse, the more your family members will follow suit.

Familial Differences

Zach and Monique came from widely different backgrounds. They could have been the poster children for the claim that "opposites attract." In terms of personalities, experiences, ethnicities, and family cultures, Zach and Monique were as different as two people could be. Despite their differences, though, these two connected instantly when friends set them up on a blind date, and they've been inseparable ever since.

Zach and Monique are both attractive people, but their chemistry was based on much more than just mutual physical attraction. In addition to a strong physical chemistry, they also bonded on much deeper levels and seemed endlessly fascinated by each other. Zach and Monique could talk for hours about any subject imaginable.

Zach and Monique always counted their differences as a source of strength in their relationship, and they never seemed uncomfortable or threatened by the areas in which they had differing opinions. They both shared a humble desire to learn from each other's perspectives, and they value each other's unique viewpoints. Differences seemed to be no problem regarding issues like restaurant preferences or even more controversial areas like politics. When Zach and Monique got married, they were fully convinced that they would never face any disagreement they couldn't resolve quickly.

Zach and Monique's life together progressed beautifully through their first years of marriage. Conflicts remained low or seemed minor even as they had their two children. Something subtly shifted, however, as their babies grew towards school age, and this young family began to have an identity crisis. All those differences that had seemed exotic and intriguing in the early years now felt threatening. Both spouses' flexibility and civility started to wane, and each family decision became an existential battle for the relationship.

As Zach and Monique paused to evaluate their situation and really talk through their issues, they realized that their greatly different upbringings were causing confusion and conflict about how their own family should operate. They had both naively assumed that they would figure things out without having to spend too much time creating clear roles and goals. Now, that lack of clarity had created a vacuum where hurt feelings and miscommunication had taken root.

Zach and Monique agreed to make a list of some of their most significant expectations based on how their parents raised them. Within a half hour, they had a handwritten document that graphically illustrated the differences in their backgrounds for the first time. Some of the points on their list reflected this huge divergence. Here are several examples:

- Zach grew up in a house in which his mother did all the cooking and cleaning. Consequently, he expected Monique to do those tasks just as his mom had. Monique grew up in a house in which her parents shared household chores, and she had always expected more partnership like that in her own marriage.

- Zach's parents disciplined him and his siblings through "time outs." Monique's parents spanked her for poor behavior, and she still believed in this form of physical discipline.

- Zach's family considered themselves Christians but only attended worship at Easter and possibly Christmas. Monique's family was at church for every event. She wanted Zach to be a spiritual leader in their home, lead the family in prayer, and prioritize church participation, but he said he didn't feel comfortable with "organized religion."

- Zach's family came from a working-class neighborhood and never had a lot of money. Monique's family was affluent, and she wanted to develop a financial plan with her husband so they could make more money, travel, save for college, and do other things. Zach was content with their financial situation and thought Monique's financial goals were elitist. She thought he lacked ambition and maybe common sense with financial matters.

- Zach's family ate almost any kind of food, loved to grill and smoke meat, and enjoyed gathering for meals. Monique's family raised her to be a vegan who ate only organic foods and no animal products. Zach didn't want to raise "weird" kids who couldn't even eat chicken nuggets. He wanted members of the family to eat whatever they wanted. Monique felt strongly that her kids should be raised with a health-focused, vegan diet.

- Zach had attended a public school. Monique had been home-schooled until she reached the ninth grade, and then she finished high school at a private academy. As their oldest child approached kindergarten, they had vastly different beliefs about what kind of educational experience their kids should have.

The more Zach and Monique talked, the larger their list grew. They uncovered differences in many other areas. They both confessed to developing some unspoken resentment towards each other over the past few years, and most of those hard feelings were rooted in the areas on their list. Contrasting opinions may have been "cute" or "intriguing" while they were dating and early in the marriage, but now those same matters had become "annoying" and "divisive."

Both Zach and Monique had to admit they had entered marriage believing their individual families had mostly done things "the right way." So anything the other spouse did that contradicted their own upbringing was "the wrong way." It also did not help that their family members felt just as strongly about their way of doing things. Some were very vocal about their opinions with the couple, which only threw gasoline on an already burning fire. The couple had to swallow a lot of pride and work through which principles were foundational and which principles were simply preferences.

Zach and Monique started the difficult work of clearly voicing their individual desires, showing respect and valuing each other's viewpoints, and striving to find common ground and shared goals for each area of their marriage and family. They also decided to look actively for the best in each other, reminding themselves daily of all the reasons they fell in love in the first place. The couple also committed to the daily work of fighting for the unity of their marriage by communicating about expectations long before they become bitter or resentful.

Although your marriage might not have as many differences as Zach and Monique had to navigate, understand that nearly every marriage will encounter some form of "culture war." Some of these disagreements are big while others are more subtle, but all these issues must be addressed with mutual respect and a desire to serve the needs of your spouse. This guideline is especially important when different upbringings combined with different personalities and preferences create a struggle between a couple.

Every marriage is different, but it is universally true that couples have to navigate one of life's constant tensions—*the desire for consistency versus the desire for change*. Both change and consistency are important aspects of life even though in their extreme forms, they are at odds with each other. On some level, we all desire predictability in our routines, yet we also crave adventure and newness to break up the monotony and predictability of life.

In many marriages, one of the most complicated disagreements is over the tension between consistency and change. Couples should have a balance, but it often turns into a battle instead. Every person is wired differently, and our own unique experiences and personalities can shape whether we have more of a desire for change or for consistency. Our families of origin have a huge impact on how we come to seek either more consistency or more change.

Watching my (Dave's) parents navigate their extreme differences in this area has taught me a lot about marriage through the years. My parents have an incredible marriage, but it's not because of compatibility. It's because of their commitment to love and learn from each other despite their differences. My parents' individual upbringings were about as opposite as anyone could imagine. Their personalities are also quite different. My mom came into the marriage with an extraordinarily strong preference for consistency while my dad longed for adventure and change. Some of these differences were hardwired into their personalities, but their families conditioned them in these ways as well.

My mom lived a simple, almost idyllic childhood. Every part of her life was structured by her family and circumstances. She grew up in the house her dad had built from a Sears Craftsman "build your own home" kit. Those were extremely popular from the early 1900s until 1942 when Sears had to stop selling them because supplies were needed for the war effort. Today, many of those homes are worth a fortune. My mom's family never moved while she was growing up. She had the same neighbors for her entire childhood because the neighbors never moved either. Dinner was at the same time every night. She went to school with all the same people, and she thrived both in and out of school. Her extended family lived nearby. She found security in the structure, and she assumed life would always have this same level of consistency.

My dad had the opposite experience. His family was constantly on the move. He began elementary school a year early so his parents could get him out of the house sooner. He ended up attending seven different elementary schools over the next six years, an average of more than one move per year. As a consequence, he never felt fully at home anywhere. He learned to be a survivor and to fit in as best as he could. He adapted to the constant changes and eventually wanted more of it. He would become restless if he were ever in the same place or doing same routine for too long.

My parents' different upbringings, preferences, and personalities collided together early in their marriage. I was born a couple weeks before their first anniversary, and they made their first cross-country move when I was still a newborn. It was the first move of Mom's life. A year later, my younger brother was born in Oklahoma. A few years after that, my youngest brother was born in Kansas City. Dad was going wherever he could find work to provide for his growing family, and Mom was working hard to create structure and consistency in the midst of all the changes.

When I was in third grade, Dad took another out-of-state job in Kentucky, and we moved once again. This move launched one of the most difficult seasons for our family and one of the most strained times in my parents' marriage. Loneliness, stress, financial pressure, culture shock, and a myriad of other factors were causing extreme tension in my parents' relationship.

There are many stories and many lessons I could recount from that era, but what stands out the most is that Mom and Dad firmly resolved together that they were going to stay united through the difficult season. They also committed to a long season of consistency for the sake of the family. For years, they had followed Dad's preference for change, but now was a time for consistency. He finally deferred to Mom's preference, and he wisely recognized it wasn't just the best thing for *her*, but it was also the best thing for the *whole family*.

My parents put down roots and built a house 33 years ago. They still live in that same house today. Even though my own personality is bent more toward change than consistency, there's such comfort in returning to their home where our family has so much history. I'm thankful for those decisions they made to put down roots all those years ago.

Mom and Dad invested in consistency for the sake of our family and their marriage, but they also made a space for change and new adventures. Once my brothers and I were grown, Dad left the consistent job he had held for more than a decade and started his own traveling consulting business. Mom wholeheartedly supported him in this new endeavor, even though the pay would now be inconsistent compared to a set salary. Dad ended up making more much money working for himself than he ever did as a "company man," but there have still been some faith-stretching, lean seasons along the way.

My parents have traveled all over the world, but they always come home to Kentucky. They have cultivated a healthy balance between consistency and change. Instead of feeling threatened by each other's differences, they have learned to celebrate each other's unique perspectives, and they have both grown a lot through the journey. Dad has grown to love the consistency they have at home. Mom has grown to love their new assignments and international travel, even though she had barely traveled outside her hometown until she was an adult.

In our own marriage, Ashley and I have had to navigate this same tension between consistency and change. Her upbringing mirrored my mom's childhood in terms of the consistency she experienced, but Ashley also had some unique adventures sprinkled in, including a two-year stint in which she and her mom lived in New York City so Ashley could pursue a career as a child actor on Broadway and in national commercials. It's true—I married a celebrity! Ashley's parents eventually decided that she and her mom needed to move back home to Kentucky because Ashley's grandfather was very ill and near the end of his life. They wanted the ability to be with him in his last days and to be available to help in any way they could. Family is always more important than any work opportunity.

Ashley and I both value consistency, but we also share a natural leaning toward change and adventure. Our desire for new adventures, as well as a hunger to pursue new opportunities for ministry, has brought about a lot of moves in our 22 years of marriage. Some of those moves have been across town to renovate a house, while others have been across the country to pursue a new work opportunity.

A few years ago, while living in Texas where **XO Marriage** is based, we sensed that our kids were not thriving, feeling connected, or being rooted in the community. We were also further from our hometown in Kentucky than we had ever been, so it was harder (and more expensive) to get home and see our extended families on any consistent basis. Our kids missed Georgia where they had primarily grown up. Our first son was born in Kentucky, but our other three sons were all born in Augusta, Georgia. After a lot of conversations, prayers, and meetings with our team, we decided to move the family back to Georgia. We wanted to give our kids the same gift our parents had given us—a consistent hometown. For the sake of our family, we knew we needed to prioritize consistency.

We still have plenty of change and adventure on our calendar. We travel regularly for work and for pleasure, too. When we are away from our kids, we work really hard to give them consistency by using the same babysitter almost every time. We've also worked to have the flexibility to be present at home as much as possible. Even as I'm working now to write these words, I'm taking frequent breaks to play with the kids or get them a snack.

Throughout the years, we've learned that change is good because it fosters growth and resilience, but consistency is also good because it builds stability and community. We need both, and each couple must navigate what having both looks like in their own marriages and families. There's not a one-size-fits-all approach. It should be a balance, not a battle. At times, your differences will lead to disagreements or even prolonged seasons of mutual frustration, but if you'll work together to find a balance, then you'll both become stronger and more unified as a result.

CHAPTER 8

Study Guide

for Individuals and Groups

Group leaders should prepare prior to the group meeting with the following steps:

- *Review Chapter 8.*
- *Read Romans 12:18.*
- *Choose one discussion question and one reflection question for group engagement in case time runs short.*
- *Pray for each group member by name. Ask the Lord to prepare their hearts and minds.*
- *If possible, silence your cell phone and remove any other distractions. Be fully present for your group and prepare to see lives transformed by God.*

Chapter 8 Summary

Jethro's positive influence as a supportive father-in-law to Moses is a practical and inspirational example for us to follow. Jethro was not a Hebrew, yet he encouraged and advised Moses at critical times during Moses's life. Moses wholeheartedly trusted Jethro's counsel because he had respect for his father-in-law and also because he knew Jethro had no secret agenda. These two men truly were gifts to each other. We believe they modeled God's ultimate plan for in-law relationships. When our relationships are rooted in acceptance and mutual respect, we too can have multigenerational family health that becomes a gift to everyone.

We should be respectful and patient with our family members' concerns. Show them respect and love. Be prepared for awkward moments and even disagreements, but don't let negative comments bring out the worst in you. Stand your ground kindly but firmly. Remind your family members that your spouse is the one you have chosen to share your life with and that you would love it if they could try to love the person you chose as well. However, if your family chooses not to love your spouse and instead engages in derogatory insults or shows disrespect toward your spouse, then you must address the situation.

Every marriage is different, but it is universally true that couples have to navigate one of life's constant tensions: *the desire for consistency versus the desire for change.* Both change and consistency are important aspects of life, even though in their extreme forms, they are at odds with each other. On some level, we all crave predictability in our routines, yet we also desire adventure and newness to break up the monotony and predictability of life. Our families of origin have an enormous impact on how we come to seek either more consistency or more change.

Throughout the years, we've learned that change is good because it fosters growth and resilience, but consistency is also good because it builds stability and community. We need both, and each couple must navigate what having both looks like in their own marriage and family.

Discussion

1. Have you received help from a parent or in-law's advice? What was the advice, and how did it help your situation?

2. Have you had to take a strong stand about the way an in-law or family member communicated with you or your spouse?

3. Do you prefer consistency or change? How does your preference compare with your spouse's?

Reflection

1. How willing are you to receive advice from a family member or in-law? What influences your willingness to hear their opinions?

2. How do you respond when a family member or in-law communicates in a way that is unacceptable? How should you respond?

3. What are some of the ways you and your spouse can come to an agreement when one of you prefers stability and other prefers change?

4. How do you respond when someone is disrespectful to your spouse? How should you respond?

Prayer

Father God, I want to have a good relationship with my parents and in-laws. Show me how to be open to advice and give me wisdom about what advice I should take. I want to be a peacemaker, but I also want to protect my spouse. Reveal to me the times when I should speak up and when I should remain silent. I want to be in unity with my spouse about all the decisions we make. Guide us when we have different opinions about issues that concern stability or change. Keep my heart soft toward my spouse as we talk about difficult issues. I trust Your Holy Spirit to guide me. In Jesus' name, Amen.

SECTION FOUR

LEGACY

And through your descendants all the nations of the earth will be blessed—all because you have obeyed me.

—Genesis 22:18

My wife comes from a long line of committed marriages, loving families, and successful people. I come from a lengthy line of divorce, addiction, and messed up people. That's an exaggerated description of both our families, but it's almost comical how different our upbringings were. Now that we're forming our own family, I want to honor both of our families even while we avoid the pitfalls my family has experienced. I want to break generational curses while not throwing away the good that my family has done. I know that they weren't perfect, but they weren't all bad either. I want to celebrate my wife's heritage without supporting the narrative that everything they've done is "perfect" because no one but God is perfect. Her family has always been good to me, but I've also felt like a charity case to them because I had a pretty rough childhood. I want to earn their respect and not just their pity. I want my wife and I to create a new family legacy that honors God and touches future generations, but I'm afraid to admit to my wife that I don't know how. I am afraid to appear helpless. I want to be a leader in my family, but I never had good examples to follow. I want to be a good example for my own kids. I also want to honor my wife's family without becoming a copy of them.

—Carl P. (Married 11 years)

CHAPTER 9

How to Love and Pray for Your In-Laws

Every family has some members who can be difficult to love. In fact, *you* can be difficult to love sometimes (and *we* can be, too). Nobody is perfect, and we all have moments when we're not at our best. For some, those unpleasant moments seem to harden into a lifestyle of unpleasantness.

When you have an in-law who seems perpetually negative or mean-spirited, it can feel as if you have an enemy living in your midst. It can seem as if you're always under attack. As a first step, we need to address our responsibility to love our difficult in-laws. Yes, you heard us right ... *love* them.

We love the Bible, but we don't understand all of it. Some parts of Scripture we read and reread, and we still scratch our heads because we have little idea what it actually means. Ironically, it's not the parts of the Bible we don't understand that bother us most, though. The parts of the Bible that really bother us are the words we do understand and simply don't like.

When Jesus gave us the command to "love your enemies" (see Matthew 5:44), there was no mistaking what He was talking about. He was clear and consistent in both His message and His actions. Jesus did not simply teach us to love our enemies—He also modeled how to do it. As Jesus was nailed to a cross, tortured to death by callous Roman soldiers, and mocked by the so-called religious elite who had put the whole execution in motion, He prayed for the very people who were killing Him.

That kind of love is usually where we draw the line. We're all for loving our friends and our lovable relatives. We even extend grace when they make mistakes, but we seldom entertain the idea of giving love to people who hate us or want to harm us. Surely Jesus didn't really mean for us to love people who treat us like that, did He?

At most, we will tolerate our enemies. "Tolerance" has become a cultural buzzword that often means we should be so open-minded as to put up with anyone's actions. But tolerance has nothing to do with love. Jesus raised the bar, because He never taught us to tolerate people. He taught us to love people. Tolerance simply masks our prejudices, but love destroys them.

The truth is, Jesus wants us to love our enemies, and it's not just for the sake of our enemies. God loves you too much to let you go through life with a heart full of bitterness. Bitterness and love can't live in the same heart, and each day you've got to decide which one gets to stay.

> Bitterness and love can't live in the same heart, and each day you've got to decide which one gets to stay.

When you love those who are hostile in return, you're doing it as an offering to God. Don't treat people the way they treat you; treat people the way God treats you. You can show respect to those who don't deserve it, not as a reflection of their character but as a reflection of yours.

The Choice Between Love and Bitterness

Jane was a peacemaker by default, but her kind nature was tested to its limit when her son married a woman who seemed determined at all costs to bring a critical and divisive spirit into the family. Over the years, Jane did her best to love her daughter-in law and be an encourager. More often than not, however, her kindness was met with coldness or unreliable behavior. Even when her daughter-in-law was being kind, Jane could not enjoy it because at any moment the switch could flip, and the kindness would turn to coldness.

Jane prayed constantly about this issue. She wanted to have a healthy relationship with her son, her daughter-in-law, and with their children, but the situation seemed broken beyond repair. Jane eventually realized her daughter-in-law's way of responding came from her broken past. Her daughter-in-law grew up in a broken family in which she experienced a great deal of rejection and hardship. Her upbringing wounded her, and whether she meant to do it or not, her wounds were now causing her to inflict pain on others.

Jane felt heartbroken over the past pain inflicted on her through her daughter-in-law's careless words and actions. Meanwhile, Jane's son seemed indifferent to it all. Jane felt abandoned, rejected, and unloved. She continued to pray for the situation to change, but it only grew worse.

A breakthrough came for Jane during a moment of desperate prayer when she was reminded of a simple but powerful truth: *Jesus loves her.* Of course, Jane knew Jesus loved her, but this reminder felt more personal and profound than anything she had experienced before. It was as if she caught a glimpse of heaven and felt the joy of knowing her heavenly Father loved her, delighted in her, and would always be there for her. Being reminded of who she is in Christ freed Jane from feeling imprisoned or helpless because of what she experienced with her son and daughter-in-law.

Jane was also able to have more compassion for her son. She began to realize that his seeming indifference was simply exhaustion over the relational tension he was feeling in his marriage. Once Jane shifted from focusing on her own pain to trying to see her son and daughter-in-law through God's eyes, she realized there were no "villains" in this story. Everyone involved was simply hurting and inadvertently hurting others.

Jane started viewing her daughter-in-law not as an enemy to be avoided or a project to be fixed but simply as a daughter to be loved and cherished. Jane made it her mission to show her daughter-in-law God's love by treating her with grace, love, service, and compassion. Jane was going to thank God daily for her daughter-in-law and ask God to reveal ways to serve her.

The relationship didn't immediately change, but Jane's perspective did. She freed herself from feeling powerless and imprisoned by the situation. Instead, she chose to give her pain to God and look for ways to serve. She chose to be thankful for the moments when things seemed to be going well in the relationship, and she also chose not to dwell on the moments when things seemed to be moving the wrong direction.

Day by day, one step, one prayer, and one conversation at a time, Jane determined she was going to keep loving her family and trusting God with the rest of the relationship. It was easier said than done, but Jane stuck with it, and it made a huge difference. Over time, some improvements took place in the family dynamics. Even more, there have been obvious improvements in Jane's peace of mind.

If you find yourself in a situation similar to Jane's, then we urge you not to lose hope. Take the pain to God. You can trust Him with it. You may need to put some boundaries in place to guard your own heart from toxic behaviors, but you may also need to shift your mind and take the focus off your own disappointments so you can start loving your wounded relatives the way God loves them.

Have the courage to be the one to go first. Have the faith to love those who are acting unlovable. Then trust God to do the rest. It may be the very thing God uses to transform your family, and at the very least, God will work through your faith to bring more peace and healing to your own heart and mind.

Loving the Unlovable

Even if no one ever puts us in a position of feeling perpetually under attack as Jane often felt, we all will eventually be called to love those whose behavior is not lovable. These opportunities are not only the most difficult but also the most important. It's really hard when relatives or in-laws are posturing more as our enemies rather than our allies.

What should we do when we have a combative, unkind, or unlovable in-law? We might find them easier to avoid than to love, and in some cases, avoidance is necessary. But God has a very special place in His heart for unlovable people, and so should we. We have to remember we are all unlovable at times.

One of our favorite stories in the Bible is in John chapter 8. This story isn't specifically about in-laws, but it is about someone many people would think is unlovable. Every verse and story has relevance if you'll look closely for the application. In this story, a woman is caught in the act of adultery, and she is dragged into the streets for a public execution. In that day and culture, it was legal to kill a woman who committed adultery. (Sadly, it is still legal in some nations today.)

The self-righteous mob was about to carry out the death sentence, and as they threw the woman onto the ground in front of Jesus, they realized they could kill two birds with one stone. They could quench their bloodlust *and* discredit Jesus by trapping Him in an unwinnable argument. Little did they know they were picking a fight with the wrong guy.

The mob gave Jesus a quick lesson on Old Testament law and explained how this woman had sinned and was worthy of death. But Jesus seemed unimpressed by their righteous indignation. Maybe it was because of the misogynistic nature of the law's enforcement. Why was only the woman to be punished? Doesn't it take *two* people to commit adultery?

Perhaps Jesus looked through their charade and saw their hypocrisy. He saw the mountain of sin in each accuser's individual life.

Maybe He looked straight at this woman and saw the brokenness of her past. He didn't just see her sin; He also saw her.

Jesus bent down and began to write something in the dirt. When He had finished, He stood and proclaimed the real truth of the situation: *"Let any one of you who is without sin be the first to throw a stone at her"* (John 8:7 NIV). One by one, the accusers dropped their stones and walked away until only Jesus and the woman remained. Jesus was the only one there without sin, and He never picked up a rock. Instead, He told the woman to go and sin no more.

Jesus offers us the same grace, and He commands us to offer that same grace and love to others. Mother Teresa once said, "If you judge people, you have no time to love them." Jesus took the time to love.

There's Always More to the Story

Another way to develop love and empathy for those difficult relatives and in-laws is to remember that their lack of kindness usually stems from a brokenness in them and not a deficiency in you. In other words, they have a story. They have pain and heartbreak. Now, that never justifies cruelty or unkindness, but once we learn where someone has been, it will often help us to have more patience and understanding about where they are now.

> Make it your mission to empathize with the difficult members of your family so you can build bridges with them.

Make it your mission to empathize with the difficult members of your family so you can build bridges with them. Be intentional as you explore ways to take interest in their stories and learn from them. As best as you are able, exhibit compassion. Here are five practical ways you can start building healthy bonds with your relatives and in-laws who may be acting in unlovable ways. These principles also apply to healthy relationships and can help them to grow even better.

1. Do not treat people the way they treat you; treat people the way God treats you.

The character of God is to give love to unlovable people. *All* of us have been unlovable by His standards, but His love makes *all* love possible. The more you love God and embrace His love and grace in your life, the more ability you will have to give love and grace to others. This single principle could transform the way you respond to your in-laws and every other person in your life. Remember, it's not about treating people the way they treat you—it's about treating them the way God treats you.

2. Invest in people at strategic low points.

Every financial advisor will tell you that if you want to maximize your investment on a security in the stock market, you need to invest in shares when the price is low, not when it is high. There are also risks in investing at low points, but that is part of the way people make money in the stock market. Relational investing has a similar principle. If you want to maximize your positive impact in someone's life, then don't invest in the relationship only when the other person is on top of the world, when they have hit their high point. Give them your best when their stock is low. Serve them when they have no way to repay you. If you are willing to stand beside them when they encounter pain and tragedy and everyone else is rushing out, then you will be a part of changing their lives, along with building a lifelong bond. That is real love.

3. Expect nothing in return.

This principle can be really hard to follow because when we give, we usually have hope that our investment will eventually have some return. However, that's not always how love works. If we only show kindness to those who will return it, then we're not showing love. We're just networking to get ahead. Give your best even when it's not reciprocated. Jesus did that for us, and He calls us to do it for others.

4. Balance tough love with compassion.

When someone we love is in a self-destructive cycle and is a potential harm to themselves or others, we must respond with tough love. Depending on the circumstances, tough love may require an intervention or even legal action, but make sure your motives are always driven by a deep and abiding compassion for the well-being of everyone involved.

5. Don't quit on them, and don't let them quit on themselves.

The Bible teaches that there is nothing we could possibly ever do to separate us from God's love (see Romans 8:38–39). God calls us to have that same limitless love for others. This love is not based on our own strength—God's strength is what makes it possible. Once someone realizes that you are going to stick with them no matter what, they can find the strength to persevere even in very difficult circumstances.

Study Guide

for Individuals and Groups

Group leaders should prepare prior to the group meeting with the following steps:

- *Review Chapter 11.*

- *Read 1 John 4:19.*

- *Choose one discussion question and one reflection question for group engagement in case time runs short.*

- *Pray for each group member by name. Ask the Lord to prepare their hearts and minds.*

- *If possible, silence your cell phone and remove any other distractions. Be fully present for your group and prepare to see lives transformed by God.*

Chapter 9 Summary

Every family has some members in it who can be difficult to love. When you have an in-law who seems perpetually negative or mean-spirited, it can feel as if you have an enemy living in your midst. As a first step, we need to address our responsibility to love our difficult in-laws.

When you love those who are hostile in return, you're doing it as an offering to God. Don't treat people the way they treat you; treat people the way God treats you. Show respect even to those who don't deserve it, not as a reflection of their character but as a reflection of yours.

Have the courage to be the one to go first. Have the faith to love those who are acting unlovable. Then trust God to do the rest. It may be the very thing God uses to transform your family, but at the very least, God will work through your faith to bring more peace and healing to your own heart and mind.

Here are five practical ways you can start building healthy bonds with your relatives and in-laws who may be acting in unlovable ways:

1. Do not treat people the way they treat you; treat people the way God treats you.

2. Invest in people at strategic low points.

3. Expect nothing in return.

4. Balance tough love with compassion.

5. Don't quit on them, and don't let them quit on themselves.

Discussion

1. When have you tried to love someone who was unlovable? What were the results?

2. Has someone shown love to you when you were unlovable? What effect did that have on your life?

3. Is there someone in your life right now to whom you need to express love and kindness—to "go first"? What steps can you take to show love to that person?

Reflection

1. Of the five practical ways to bond with a difficult in-law, which one inspires you the most? Why did you choose your answer?

2. How can you more effectively balance tough love with compassion?

3. Is there someone in your life right now whom you want to quit on? How will you resist that urge and pray for them instead?

Prayer

Father God, I admit some people in my life seem unlovable. I need Your guidance as I relate to them. I confess I have not always followed Jesus' example in my love for others. I ask You to forgive me and teach me to love as You do. Please help me manage my thoughts and feelings regarding those who have done hurtful things to me or those I love. I cannot do this on my own. I trust You to help me become the person You want me to be. In Jesus' name, Amen.

How to Be a Great In-Law

We've shared several negative examples of in-law relationships that have gone haywire, but obviously, our goal is to help everyone create more positive examples. We want to be good in-laws, and we want to equip others to do the same. We can learn from the negative examples, but there is much more to learn from the positive ones.

Whether we are discussing ways to be great in-laws to the older generation ahead or the younger generation behind, all positive examples have one key component in common: *love.* A great in-law loves truly and wholeheartedly. They also make sure their in-laws and other family members know that they love them. It is important for us to clarify that love is not merely a feeling. Even if you're having a hard time "feeling" affectionate toward your in-laws, you can still choose to love them. We believe your feelings will usually catch up to your actions. *Eventually.*

It is possible for us to become truly loving because we are made in the image of God, and God, by definition, is love. His love is rooted in commitment. If we were to say, "I love you" to someone, then we are not simply expressing our current feelings; we are also making a commitment for our shared future. Love, by its very nature, is a conscious choice to selflessly put the needs of someone else ahead of our own preferences or comforts. No relationship can survive unless it is rooted in rock-solid commitment.

10 Biblical Character Traits for Healthy In-Law Relationships

The Bible supplies 10 important character traits to illustrate the kind of commitment we should have in our relationships. If you have the desire to be a great in-law, then start by committing to these healthy traits. Even if these traits aren't being reciprocated by your in-laws, be consistent with your example. You might become a force for good and change for the entire family.

1. Respect

Show proper respect to everyone.

—1 Peter 2:17 NIV

Healthy in-laws show respect regardless of their differences of opinion. They honor the sanctity and independence of every individual and every marriage within the larger family. They don't push boundaries or play mind games to move their own agenda forward. They're willing to show deference and respect to everyone for the sake of harmony and peace.

2. Generosity

God loves a cheerful giver.

—2 Corinthians 9:7 NIV

Healthy in-laws are joyfully generous with no strings attached to their generosity. We don't necessarily mean financial generosity, because some family members may never be in a position to offer any financial assistance or give expensive holiday gifts. Generosity is a mindset that includes being generous with time, service, and flexibility, both during the holidays and throughout everyday life. Generous in-laws give with no agenda other than wanting to be a blessing.

3. Humility

God opposes the proud but gives grace to the humble.

—James 4:6

Healthy in-laws admit fault, apologize for mistakes, and learn new ways of doing things. When they have blown it, they own it, and they work to rebuild trust. They have confidence without pride. Their confidence rests in the assurance and identity they have in Christ. Pride tempts us to think we are our own god who doesn't answer to anyone else but ourselves. Pride destroys families. Humility heals families.

4. Encouragement

Encourage one another and build each other up.

—1 Thessalonians 5:11 NIV

Healthy in-laws are your cheerleaders, not your critics. Their applause is not only for their blood relatives but also for those who have entered the family through marriage. They build others up with their words and actions. They want you to win in all parts of life.

5. Flexibility

I can do all things through Christ who strengthens me.

—Philippians 4:13 NKJV

Healthy in-laws don't assume their way of doing things is the *only* way. They do are not rigid with their schedule or even their traditions. They are always thoughtful towards everyone involved, and they make plans with the goal of accommodating everyone.

6. Grace

Be kind and compassionate to one another, forgiving each other, just as in Christ God forgave you.

—Ephesians 4:32 NIV

Every family needs forgiveness. People will hurt other people's feelings. In every situation, grace must flow freely. Healthy in-laws live grace-filled lives. This doesn't mean they are doormats or pushovers, but it does mean they are quick to forgive and not prone to hold grudges.

7. Gratitude

Give thanks in all circumstances; for this is God's will for you in Christ Jesus.

—1 Thessalonians 5:18 NIV

Healthy in-laws have no sense of entitlement. Instead, they have hearts of gratitude. They say "thank you" often and with sincerity. They communicate their gratefulness for you and for the unique contributions you make. They will let you know how thankful they are that you have joined the family.

8. Hospitality

Always be eager to practice hospitality.

—Romans 12:13

Healthy in-laws are happy to host you. They do everything within their power to make sure you feel welcomed in their home. They treat your presence like an honor and not a burden.

9. Honesty

An honest answer is like a kiss on the lips.

—Proverbs 24:26 NIV

Healthy in-laws are always honest, but they speak the truth with love. They do not gossip behind your back. They do not deceive you. They are straightforward, transparent, and truthful in their communication.

10. Love

And do everything with love.

—1 Corinthians 16:14

More than anything else, healthy in-laws are loving. The Bible says, "Love covers a multitude of sins" (1 Peter 4:8). Every family has issues, but when love is the driving force, it is enough to cover our imperfections. Love is much more than affectionate feelings. Love is a commitment, a selfless choice to put others ahead of ourselves.

Changing the Communication Dynamic

We might think we are already doing a decent job of implementing the list above, but everyone has blind spots. I (Dave) had a blind spot recently that Ashley lovingly helped me correct. We were walking through the aisles of a large department store when she put her arm around me and placed something into the cart. Ashley lovingly whispered in my ear, "Trust me. It is time for this."

I looked down into the cart and saw that the item she had placed there was an electric nose hair trimmer. I laughed at first thinking it was a joke, but then I discreetly reached up to my upper lip to discover that indeed I had the beginnings of a mustache emerging from my nostrils! My wife helped me see a blind spot.

Some blind spots are as innocuous as a few unsightly nose hairs, while others can be less visible but far more dangerous. When our habits, mindsets, or choices start to veer off course in an unhealthy direction, a wise spouse helps us see the situation from a new perspective. A loving spouse will tell you the truth, even when it may be a difficult to hear. Tenderhearted transparency is an often-overlooked secret to lifelong love. This advice is not simply great for marriages; it is also great for how to be a healthy in-law.

Some people master the art of "honesty," but they have no tenderness. They act as if criticism is a spiritual gift. For the record, criticism is *not* a spiritual gift, but encouragement is still on the list. A critical in-law will use their so-called honesty as a weapon to wound their relatives. They hurl corrective insults from a posture of power as if it were their job to correct, shape, or referee every aspect of others' lives. They are fluent in the languages of nagging, criticism, and sarcasm.

Other in-laws are great at tenderness, but they forget transparency. They are afraid of awkward conversations, so they hold back on the honesty. They pretend issues do not really exist. They seem incapable of sharing the whole truth. They always are saying everything is "fine," but for them, "F.I.N.E" really means they are Faking, Ignoring, Neglecting, and Evading the real issues.

In our family, Ashley and I both overused the word "fine" in the past so we could avoid talking about how we were really feeling. We believed the myth that we should be able to read each other's mind and perfectly interpret nonverbal cues, which would let us know when something really was *not* fine. When the other failed to notice these telepathic messages, we would become frustrated, which would then lead to arguments. This exhausting cycle continued until we finally found the courage to share what was really on our hearts and minds, and it changed everything for the better.

Perhaps you have struggled with communication in your relationship like we did. The good news is that you do not have to stay stuck in a negative cycle, and better yet, you do not have to figure out the solution on your own. The Bible gives us a proven recipe for healthy communication. God's Word is the world's best resource for healthy relationships.

The apostle Paul wrote this about our communication:

> Instead, we will speak the truth in love, growing in every way more and more like Christ, who is the head of his body, the church (Ephesians 4:15).

We should always be honest, and simultaneously, we should always be loving. Truth and love can be a difficult tightrope to navigate, but we must choose to live in the tension of being 100 percent honest and 100 percent loving. Later in the same chapter, Paul gave these instructions:

> Get rid of all bitterness, rage, anger, harsh words, and slander, as well as all types of evil behavior. Instead, be kind to each other, tenderhearted, forgiving one another, just as God through Christ has forgiven you (Ephesians 4:31–32).

Those two verses contain powerful and practical instruction for churches and families, but we can still feel overwhelmed about knowing where to start, especially when we have fallen into a negative communication cycle with our in-laws. It takes a lot of courage to be the one to *go first* when we are trying to change a relationship dynamic. Here are a few practical steps you can take to help you get started:

1. Take an inventory of your vocabulary and remove words that are not helpful.

Some unhelpful words are easy for us to spot. Using curse words with your family members obviously has no place, so get rid of profanities, but don't stop there. Also commit to removing critical words, sarcastic words, and ambiguous words, such as *fine*. These words can do more harm than good. Make sure your words communicate your love and commitment to each other. You should remove from your vocabulary any words that are harming your family.

2. Commit to complete honesty and transparency.

Tell the truth, but always speak it in love. Do not use the truth as a weapon to hurt your in-laws. Speak with tenderness and compassion and never deceit.

3. Learn the difference between discretion and deception.

Sometimes the wisest thing to say is nothing at all. Not every thought that enters your head needs to be shared or said aloud. Certainly, we should err on the side of sharing what is on our hearts, but when the words could be critical or hurtful, the discretion to remain silent and process your thoughts before speaking is the wisest choice. Have the discretion to choose words wisely, but do not ever be deceptive by refusing to confess a sin or by concealing what is really on your heart.

4. Give a lot of grace to your spouse and a lot of grace to yourself too.

The last section of these verses we shared from Ephesians is all about forgiveness. Refuse to keep score of each other's faults, and instead, be quick to forgive and seek forgiveness. When you and your family choose to be full of grace, then your relationships with your in-laws can be some of the most enjoyable relationships in your life.

Study Guide

for Individuals and Groups

Group leaders should prepare prior to the group meeting with the following steps:

- *Review Chapter 10.*

- *Read Proverbs 24:26; Romans 12:13; and Ephesians 4:2, 15, 31–32.*

- *Choose one discussion question and one reflection question for group engagement in case time runs short.*

- *Pray for each group member by name. Ask the Lord to prepare their hearts and minds.*

- *If possible, silence your cell phone and remove any other distractions. Be fully present for your group and prepare to see lives transformed by God.*

Chapter 10 Summary

Whether we are discussing ways to be great in-laws to the older generation ahead or the younger generation behind, all positive

examples have one key component in common: *love.* A great in-law
loves truly and wholeheartedly. It is possible for us to become truly
loving because we are made in the image of God, and God, by definition, is love. His love is rooted in commitment. No relationship
can survive unless it is rooted in rock-solid commitment.

The Bible supplies some important character traits to illustrate
the kind of healthy commitment we should have. The following
10 character traits are biblical, and we have listed them in no particular order.

1. Respect
2. Generosity
3. Humility
4. Encouragement
5. Flexibility
6. Grace
7. Gratitude
8. Hospitality
9. Honesty
10. Love

Tenderhearted transparency is an often-overlooked secret to
lifelong love. Some people master the art of "honesty," but they
have no tenderness. Other in-laws are great at tenderness, but they
forget transparency. Perhaps you have struggled with communication in your relationship. The good news is you do not have to
stay stuck in a negative cycle. Thankfully, you also do not have to
figure out the solution on your own. The Bible gives us a proven
recipe for healthy communication. God's Word is the world's best
resource for healthy relationships.

The apostle Paul wrote this about our communication:

Instead, we will speak the truth in love, growing in every way more and more like Christ, who is the head of his body, the church (Ephesians 4:15).

Later in the same chapter, Paul gave these instructions:

Get rid of all bitterness, rage, anger, harsh words, and slander, as well as all types of evil behavior. Instead, be kind to each other, tenderhearted, forgiving one another, just as God through Christ has forgiven you (Ephesians 4:31–32).

Those two verses contain powerful and practical instruction for churches and families, but we can still feel overwhelmed about knowing where to start, especially when we have fallen into a negative communication cycle with our in-laws. It takes a lot of courage to be the one to *go first* when we are trying to change a relationship dynamic. Here are a few practical steps you can take to help you get started:

1. Take an inventory of your vocabulary and remove words that are not helpful.
2. Commit to complete honesty and transparency.
3. Learn the difference between discretion and deception.
4. Give a lot of grace to your spouse and a lot of grace to yourself too.

Discussion

1. Which of the 10 biblical character traits are most prominent in your relationships? Which traits would you like to see more of?
2. What does *tenderhearted transparency* mean to you?
3. Have you ever known someone who practiced tenderhearted transparency? How would you describe that person?

Reflection

1. Of the four ways to change your communication dynamics, which one needs the most work in your life? Which one are you most successfully practicing right now? Give an example.

2. What would it look like to give your spouse and yourself grace today?

3. Have you ever struggled with negative vocabulary? Are you struggling right now? What do you think is the best way to change the words you use?

Prayer

Father God, Your Word is my guide. Help me to follow the Bible as I communicate with my spouse, family members, and in-laws. I do not always use my tongue to speak the right words. Guide the things I do and speak. I want my words to communicate life and hope. I want to give and forgive as Jesus did. I ask Your Holy Spirit to guide me as I follow Jesus' example. In Jesus' name, Amen.

Conclusion

Speak the truth in love. Be honest and vulnerable in every situation. Be each other's biggest encouragers. Practice tenderhearted transparency. If you will do these things with consistency, then you will be amazed by the positive difference they will make in your own attitude and in your relationships with your in-laws.

You might not feel connection or affection with certain in-laws. In fact, they might be downright difficult to love, but instead of focusing on the negative, think about the reasons you must love and honor these family members who are now in your life. First, *God has asked you to do it.* That is really the only reason you need. Second, by loving them, *you are honoring your spouse, you are creating the opportunity for a healthy multi-generational family, and you're allowing God to sanctify some of your own selfishness in the process.*

We understand this process is not always simple. Some people are easy to love, but others may be difficult because of their own issues or the way they have hurt you or your spouse. To rid ourselves of extra burdens and difficult people, we might allow our pride to get in the way and cause us to say or think things such as the following:

- "I married you, not your family! I am not responsible for them."

- "I would respect your family if they would just act respectable and show respect to me."

- "I'll start helping them when they start helping us."
- "I didn't sign up for this!"

Certainly, we can experience times when healthy boundaries with in-laws need to be set up for reasons we've discussed throughout this book. However, one challenge we should embrace is to stop focusing only on the negative and start yielding to God's plan. Instead of begging God to remove someone from your life, we should start praying, "Lord, please help me love this person the way You love them. Help me see them through Your eyes. Help me show them Your love and grace by how I treat them."

Lord, please help me love this person the way You love them.

That prayer is not always easy for us to pray, and it is not an effortless prayer to live out. If you will truly surrender these difficult relationships into God's hands, then He will always do something beautiful. Again, it will not always be easy. In fact, chances are high that it will be difficult, and improvements will come slowly and painfully. Do not give up! God is with you in this struggle.

Two Words That Changed Our Lives

I (Dave) have never heard God audibly speak, but years ago, I received what I believe was a "text message from God" in a very unlikely way. This two-word message gave me hope, and I pray it does the same for you. In fact, these two words might be the two most important words in the whole book and the message God wants you to remember more than any other.

We had recently moved our family to a new city, and I was serving as a pastor in a new church. The transitions and pressures of life and ministry with a young family were beginning to overwhelm me. I felt exhausted, misunderstood, frustrated, discouraged, and near the end of my rope. I wanted to quit. Every part of life was difficult. Things were hard at work and at home. With the many miles between us and our extended families, life was getting difficult in those relationships as well.

I was venting about all my headaches and heartaches to Ashley one night while she patiently listened. Finally, in frustration, I stood up from the couch and began to stomp around the living room like a toddler in protest. I said, *"God, it feels like You are being completely quiet right now! Where are You? I could really use a message from You. Just tell me what I am supposed to do here! If You will just tell me what to do, I will do it."*

I plopped back on the couch in frustration and threw my feet up on the ottoman. Ashley looked down at my foot and said, "You've got something stuck on your foot."

I looked down at a sticker on my heel. As I peeled it off to look at it, I had to catch my breath because what it said overwhelmed me. I was (and still am) convinced that sticker on my foot was as clear a message from God as I have ever received. It simply said, ***"KEEP GOING!"***

That experience marked a turning point in my attitude and perspective. I wrote the date "6-30-10" on that sticker and placed it on the front page of my Bible as a constant reminder to "Keep Going." God gave me the strength to press through that difficult season, and eventually, almost every area of life began to improve. Things did not become simple or easy, but with a new resolve to move forward, everything became more manageable, and we were reminded that God was with us through every step of the journey.

We have all had moments when we have felt as though we wanted to give up. We have all experienced times when we have wondered where God was in everything. Maybe you are in one of those moments right now in your marriage, your family, or life in general. We pray that you will remember God is with you. He is for you, He will carry you through the struggle, He will bring purpose from your pain, and He will reward your faithfulness.

Do not give up! Keep going. Jesus is with you, and He will never leave you or forsake you. He has a beautiful plan for your family, including your in-laws.

And let us run with endurance the race God has set before us. We do this by keeping our eyes on Jesus, the champion who initiates and perfects our faith (Hebrews 12:1–2).

Some Frequently
Asked Questions

We hope this book has answered your questions for your unique family situation, but as an added resource, we want to share a few of the most common scenarios we have received related to in-laws. Here are some questions and our answers to each one:

My daughter is seriously dating a young man who does not seem to be good for her. We don't think they are a good match, but I am hesitant to say anything. If they do get married, then I don't want him to think we were against him, and I obviously don't want our daughter to pull away from us. It feels like we are in a no-win situation! What should we do?

Your situation is indeed a delicate and common one. By saying too much, you could alienate yourselves from both of them. By saying too little, you could have major regrets if they eventually get married and then encounter the very challenges you thought they might face.

For starters, we would recommend that you avoid making definitive statements that could come back to haunt you, such as, "He's just not right for you" or "You could do so much better." These declarations might sum up exactly how you feel, but if this young man becomes your son-in-law and eventually learns you have said these things, then it could create lifelong distrust and resentment in the relationship.

Instead of focusing on your issues with him, lovingly point out some specific areas where they are struggling and offer solutions. Tell your daughter that you love her and will wholeheartedly welcome this man into the family if she chooses him to be her husband, but every relationship takes hard work and you have noticed some challenges in their relationship that could become bigger with marriage. Tell her that getting married will not *fix* those issues, but it is likely to make them more difficult unless they are resolved before marriage.

Instead of warning your daughter against marrying this young man, encourage her to resolve all those issues before marriage. Offer to help pay for premarital counseling with a professional who can help them see their blind spots. We also have created a premarital course available at www.premarriage.com with self-guided questions and resources that engaged and seriously dating couples can ask each other, which could help them determine whether they are a healthy match and ready to begin a healthy marriage.

In addition to all of this, pray! Ask God to guide your daughter's steps. If this relationship is unhealthy, pray for the Lord to let your daughter see the truth so her own feelings and affections do not blind her about this man. Also, pray for this young man. Pray that he would become the man God intends him to be so that he can be a wonderful husband and father someday whether he marries your daughter or not.

Our son has been married for two years, and we barely see him, but he and his wife spend a lot of time with her family. They prioritize the wife's family for holidays and other days too. It feels like we always get the leftovers or get nothing at all. Once grandchildren start arriving, this dynamic is going to be even more heartbreaking! How can we express our concerns without alienating them?

It can feel like an impossible situation when married children choose to spend a disproportionate amount of time with the other side of the family while neglecting yours. Addressing it can be delicate because we are sure you don't want to push them further away. Still, you will need to address this issue.

For starters, keep inviting them to specific events. Ask them to come to everything from meals to hangouts to vacations. When they do show up, be as kind, encouraging, and generous as you can be. Create an inviting and life-giving environment that draws them in. Give as much as you can give without asking for anything in return, and do not scold or shame them when they cannot attend.

Another way to build a relational bond is to look for ways to serve them. Asking them to come and hang out with you on your terms is essentially asking them to serve you, but when you take the lead in serving them, it may open many new opportunities for time together. Ask what needs they have. Offer to help paint that room they want to redo in their home. Offer to serve them in practical ways. Those small acts of service could build lasting bonds.

When you have done all those things consistently and there is still an obvious disparity in the time they spend with you, then address it with your son. Tell him that you love him and his wife, and you want to have a great relationship with them and with your future grandchildren. Point out the pattern that appears as though they are avoiding your side of the family. Instead of making demands, ask what you can do to create a better environment for them to want to join. Finally, if it is possible, invite your son's in-laws to some gatherings or out to dinner. You don't have to be best friends, but they should feel as though you support their relationship with their daughter and your son.

My husband's parents spoil our children. They are sweet and generous people, but when our kids are with them, there are no rules, and the kids get whatever they want. By the time the kids get home, it takes us days to "detox" them from their sugar highs and get them back into a regular routine. We have made subtle remarks about how the kids behave after time with the grandparents, but my in-laws just laugh about it. I am thankful my husband's parents are so supportive and generous, but how can I express my concerns without hurting my relationship with them?

Start by focusing on the positive. Instead of looking at all the ways the grandparents are spoiling the children and making life more complicated, focus on the facts that the grandparents are generous and loving and that they want to be present. Those are great things! When you start with the positive, it can help reframe the whole situation.

Give the grandparents some grace. In many ways, they have earned the right to spoil their grandkids. Yes, boundaries are important in all relationships, but take the pressure off yourself to feel as though you must rigidly rule over everything that happens at Grandma and Grandpa's house. It is okay that the rules there are a little bit different from the rules at your place. You will probably want to spoil your own grandkids someday.

With that said, you still have a right and a responsibility to enforce whatever rules and overall principles you feel strongly about. If the grandparents are completely dismissive of your rules and requests, then you may need to let them know that they are choosing to be less present in their grandkids' lives. While you want them to be present and you're truly thankful for all they do, there still must be some basic ground rules.

You are the parents. You are the ultimate decisionmakers. You are the ones who will give an account for how you raised your children. Your decision-making authority must be respected by the children and also by the grandparents.

When any type of "corrective" conversation needs to happen with the grandparents, the adult child of those grandparents (in this case, your husband) should lead. He should address his parents and point out the boundaries that need to be implemented. By him taking the lead in that, he will be protecting your relationship with your in-laws.

_____

My mother-in-law wants to move in with us. She is still healthy enough to live independently, but she likes having people do everything for her. However, I am afraid that if she lives here, then it will wear us out physically and financially. I love her and want to support her, but I do not feel good about her living here. Should we let her move in, or should we find an alternative even if she does not like it?

Most couples will face some version of this scenario in their lifetimes. It can be difficult to decide how to care best for an aging parent. We do have a responsibility to care for aging parents, but we also have a responsibility to protect our own marriages and our mental health. It can be stressful and confusing when those responsibilities seem to conflict with one another.

In this scenario, the first step is to get to a place of unity with your spouse about the issue. Pray together. Talk through all the options. Decide as a couple what would be best and then move forward.

If you decide it would be best for your mother-in-law to move in, then plan to create an environment where she can have independence and private space, and you and your spouse can also have the same. Adjust as you do whatever is necessary to make the situation as sustainable and enjoyable as possible for everyone involved.

If you decide that your mother-in-law should not move in, then supply alternative solutions. Help her not to feel rejected by the decision. Let her know that after discussing all the options and looking at your own current lifestyle and homelife, better options are available. Give her choices and dignity to be able to make as many decisions as possible about what is best for herself. Do whatever you can to help her find what she needs.

_____

My husband works for his parents in a family business. Family surrounds us constantly, and every part of our lives (and our finances)

*has a family tie. I feel like we do not have any privacy or indepen-
dence. I wish my husband would take a different job, but he wants
to take over the family business someday. Plus, if he quits, then it
might cause permanent damage to his relationship with his parents. What should we do?*

Working with family can be a blessing, but it can also create
many complications. It is a beautiful legacy to create and grow a
business that you can hand to your children someday, but parents must hold loosely to those kinds of dreams, because God's
dreams for your children might be different from yours. We must
each have the freedom to do what we feel is best for our own
marriages and callings without fear of losing a parent's love or
blessing because of our decisions.

You and your husband must decide together what is best for
your marriage and family. After praying and talking through the
options, you might produce a plan that keeps him in the family
business but also puts boundaries in place to make sure you both
have more freedom, autonomy, and privacy without feeling bombarded by extended family issues. You may choose a different
direction and decide he needs to branch off into a new career field
or even a new town.

Whatever you decide, it must be what is best for your marriage
even if it is not what is best for your in-laws' family business. We
are called to honor our parents, but in adulthood, that does not
mean obeying them. Sometimes your decisions are going to be the
best thing for you, but they could still disappoint your parents (or
in-laws) and that is okay.

Right now, it sounds like you and your husband are not unified
on this issue. The first and most important step is to work together
to find a unified solution. Keep talking. Keep praying. Seek outside
counseling if necessary. If you are still having trouble finding unity on
this issue or any issue in marriage, then we encourage you connect
with one of our Marriage Mediators at www.xomarriage.com/help.

We raised my daughter to follow Jesus, but she married a man who is not a believer, and now faith does not seem to be part of their lives. They are raising their kids outside the church, and it is heartbreaking for us. How should we respond?

We have some good friends who have found themselves in this exact scenario. They have responded by looking for every opportunity to serve their daughter's family and show the love of Jesus in practical ways. They have volunteered to watch the kids as often as they can, and when they are with their grandchildren, they make sure to talk to them about God's love, introduce them to Christian music, and take them to church activities.

They have also worked to build a good relationship with their son-in-law. They share faith with him without coming across as judgmental or "preachy." They pray for him and for the whole family. They love wholeheartedly. Love is always the first step in pointing someone to God.

Pray for your daughter's family and do your best to share your faith with them in authentic ways. Also, free yourself from the pressure of feeling like their eternal destination is somehow on your shoulders. God loves your daughter's family even more than you do. Find peace in His love and His plan. Do what you can do and trust God with the rest.

We are currently estranged from my spouse's parents. They have been very manipulative in the past, and I am hesitant to pursue restoration with them because, honestly, our lives are much easier without them in the picture. What should I do?

Some situations make it impossible to have a healthy relationship because the other people involved refuse to make healthy choices. In scenarios such as these, estrangement may be the only possibility for a period of time, or in extreme cases, the permanent solution.

You say it would be easier to keep living without them in the picture, and that may be true. But the bigger question is, "What is the best option?" Sometimes what is easiest and what is best are two different matters.

Free yourself from having to navigate this situation all on your own. We encourage you and your spouse to start by meeting with a Christian counselor. Stay focused on finding healing and unity around this specific issue with your spouse's parents. Through prayer, counseling, and discussions with your spouse, decide as a couple what is the best course of action.

If you decide to pursue healing in this relationship, then reach out to your spouse's parents. A safe first step may be to send them a letter. Writing out a letter helps you organize your thoughts and words with clarity. Let them know you wish for healing in the relationship. Also, tell them you love them and are praying for them. Invite them to join you in family counseling or family mediation.

Remember, there is nothing so broken that God cannot fix it. What seems impossible in human terms is always possible with Him. We are praying for you and with you and believing that healing and restoration will happen.

What resources do you recommend for blended families or multi-cultural families?

For blended families, we recommend *Blended and Redeemed* (book and study guide) by Scott and Vanessa Martindale, as well as *Blending Families* (book and workbook) by Jimmy Evans. Scott, Vanessa, and Jimmy have all written articles about important blended family issues, and these articles are available to read for free on www.xomarriage.com. You can also learn more about Scott and Vanessa's ministry to blended families at www.blendedkingdomfamilies.com.

For multi-cultural families, Luis and Kristen Román offer an incredible workshop titled "Multicultural Marriage & In-Laws." Being raised in different cultures, Luis and Kristen know the challenges and blessings of adapting to different families. In this workshop, they share practical tips and advice on how to bring together families of different cultures. This workshop is available on XO Marriage's streaming platform called XO Now, and the XO Now app is available for Android, iPhone, iPad, Apple TV, Chromecast, Roku, and Fire TV.

Thank you for entrusting us with your questions. If you have specific questions that we did not answer in this book, then please feel free to reach out to us anytime. You can contact us through our website at www.DaveAndAshleyWillis.com or on Instagram @DaveAndAshleyWillis.

Quick Lists

With the purchase of this book, you are granted permission to make copies of the lists on the following pages. These lists are some of the most helpful summaries of the content in this book. We hope you will share them in your church, with your friends, and with your family as you tell others about how this book has helped you in your relationships.

10 Biblical Traits to Guide In-Law Relationships

In 1 Corinthians 13:4–7, the apostle Paul mentions 10 biblical traits that should guide our relationships. We have applied them to the in-law relationship.

1. Be patient with yourself, your spouse, your in-laws, and even God as you navigate making these relationships stronger and healthier.

2. Always speak and act kindly toward your in-laws and speak kindly about them to others.

3. Resist the urge to be jealous of your in-laws.

4. Be willing to listen to what your in-laws have to say and do not let pride keep you from doing so.

5. Show respect and honor to your in-laws by caring about their perspectives.

6. Be willing to compromise at times and do your best to pursue peace for all parties.

7. Assume the best of your in-laws but also be willing to address issues in a healthy way when they arise.

8. Fight against resentment by being honest with your spouse about any issues.

9. Protect your marriage and the peace in your home by collaborating with your spouse to create healthy boundaries with your extended family.

10. Keep praying for your marriage and family and hold onto the hope that God is the God of restoration and peace.

© 2023 by Dave and Ashley Willis, *Married into the Family*. Used by permission. All rights reserved.

What Does It Mean to "Leave and Cleave"?

This explains why a man leaves his father and mother and is joined to his wife, and the two are united into one.

—Genesis 2:24

God's vision for marriage requires *three distinct steps:*

1. Leave the family of origin.

We consciously choose to break off from our original roots and replant a combined root in new soil with our new spouse. We stay rooted in God. Ideally, our family and community will support this new life with a new spouse.

2. Join and unite together.

This process requires faith and complete commitment. It is the deliberate act of letting go of every other earthly bond so we will be able to embrace our spouse completely and wholeheartedly with a level of intimacy and commitment above all other people or things.

3. Embrace complete commitment and nakedness.

God Himself supernaturally completes this last step. He makes two individuals into "one flesh." God creates a spiritual unity, which mingles our very souls together. We still, of course, keep our individual identities, but now and for the rest of our lives, we are tied together with a bond of love only God could have orchestrated. That is marriage. That is real intimacy. It is what God intends for you and your spouse.

© 2023 by Dave and Ashley Willis, *Married into the Family*. Used by permission. All rights reserved.

10 Unhealthy Types of In-Laws

1. **The Bullies**

   Bullying in-laws use their power to belittle, manipulate, criticize, intimidate, and control others. They must be given clear boundaries because without boundaries, they will inflict unmendable damage upon your marriage and family.

2. **The Judges**

   Driven by the need to maintain control, judges make the rules and set the standards. They will attempt to make you and your spouse play by their self-created rules, occasionally letting you know when you have succeeded but always informing you when you have failed.

3. **The Elitists**

   Elitists tend to look down on others. They might subtly or obviously let you know you are lucky to be associated with their family. They may even communicate that you will never truly be part of their family.

4. **The Takers**

   Takers will always try to take whatever they can get. If you have financial means, then they'll want your generosity at every turn. If you don't have a lot of money, then they'll push for other things, like access to you or time with your kids.

5. **The Scorekeepers**

   Scorekeepers always keep a tally. You will always feel as though you are losing on their scorecard even if you don't know the game that is being played.

6. **The Gaslighters**
Gaslighters constantly rewrite history and redefine reality to give themselves the upper hand in relationships. They try to make anyone who disagrees with them question their own judgment. In the worst cases, gaslighters' targets start to feel as though they are crazy.

7. **The Separators**
Separators constantly seem to want to divide you and your spouse. They want to put a wedge between you and your spouse so they can keep control over their "child" without your interference.

8. **The Smotherers**
Smotherers are usually operating out of sweet and selfless motives. But when one or both of your in-laws is a helper by nature, they may go overboard with the desire to help.

9. **The Chemically Imbalanced**
The chemically imbalanced may struggle with chemical addiction to drugs or alcohol, or they may have other physical issues that require medication. Encouraging necessary medications can be a delicate conversation and also might eventually require some sort of intervention.

10. **The Ghosts**
Ghosts intentionally vanish from your life. Contact becomes less and less frequent until you are not part of each other's lives at all anymore.

© 2023 by Dave and Ashley Willis, *Married into the Family*. Used by permission. All rights reserved.

5 Out-of-Bounds Behaviors

1. **Ignoring your spouse**
   Some people ignore their spouses when they don't get their way as a means of punishing them. Others ignore their spouses simply to avoid talking about hard issues. Whatever the motivation, we shouldn't avoid our spouses or emotionally shut them out of our lives.

2. **Speaking negatively about your spouse to other people, including family members**
   If you have an issue with your spouse, then you must address the problem directly with your spouse. Nothing good will come from going to friends or family members about a problem that you really need to work through with your spouse.

3. **Allowing other people to speak negatively about your spouse**
   You should never allow your family, friends, or anyone else to speak negatively about your spouse. If you have this kind of experience, then you can put to a stop to it by kindly saying, "Please don't talk about my spouse that way." It is as simple as that.

4. **Keeping secrets from one another**
   When we keep secrets of any kind from each other, we limit the amount of intimacy we can experience with our spouse. If you keep secrets from your spouse, even if they are between you and your family members, you are in dangerous territory.

5. **Speaking unkindly or shouting at one another**
   It is not okay to speak in a nasty tone, use harsh language, or scream and shout at one another. We don't have a license to give our spouses a tongue-lashing. In fact, we made a promise to love our spouses through the good times and the bad times.

© 2023 by Dave and Ashley Willis, *Married into the Family*. Used by permission. All rights reserved.

In-Law Relationship Questions

- How do we honor the legacies of both families yet still create our own unique legacy?
- How do we honor both families' values when parts of the value systems seem broken?
- Which parts of our individual upbringings do we want to transfer to our own family and children? Which aspects do we never want to carry on?
- How will we defend each other if a parent or relative shows disrespect or becomes controlling over our lives or the lives of our children?
- How can we build a strong, lifelong bond with our parents while we keep healthy boundaries that protect our marriage and family?
- How should we divide our time and the holidays between both families in a fair and balanced way? How will we defend our choices if challenged?
- How can we offer helpful critiques about some parts of each other's upbringings without coming across as disrespectful or judgmental toward our respective families?
- What does it mean for us to "leave and cleave" as the Bible teaches? Will it require us to move away from our families so we can build a strong marriage and family of our own?
- How much help can or should we give if a parent or relative needs physical or financial support?
- How can we support a healthy relationship between our kids and our parents even if we have a strained relationship with our parents?
- As our own children get married and we become the "in-laws," how should we nurture healthy behaviors and avoid unhealthy ones?
- What should we do to build a healthy, multi-generational legacy that includes faith, love, and shared values?

© 2023 by Dave and Ashley Willis, *Married into the Family*. Used by permission. All rights reserved.

In-Law Boundary Questions

- How many days a week do we need to be in contact with our parents?

- Once we agree on frequency, how can we achieve it? Do we make phone calls, send texts, organize family dinners, or plan visits? What will be our mix?

- What is the biggest concern we have with our parents now?

- What steps can we take to ease some feelings of tension for both us and our parents? Can we make some schedule changes? Would an honest conversation to directly address the issues help? Should we consider spending a little less time with our parents in the short term? Do we need to make any apologies? How can we offer forgiveness even if no apology has been offered?

- Do we feel that our parents are disregarding any of our boundaries? If so, what is best way for us to address this issue with them? Should we call, send a text, or sit down and discuss the issue over a meal? Should one or both of us address the boundary issue? Which would be most effective and lead to a healthier relationship?

- Have either of us crossed our parents' boundaries? If so, how should we discuss the issue with them and make it right?

© 2023 by Dave and Ashley Willis, *Married into the Family*. Used by permission. All rights reserved.

3 Categories of Disagreements

Principle Issues

Principle issues include commitments, such as those to each other, to your children, to a core set of values, or to having healthy in-law relationships. These issues are so foundational to a marriage that a disagreement becomes tantamount to divorce and may lead to one. In areas of principle, you must fight for the unity of your marriage. Even if your opinions differ slightly over how you should live out principle commitments, you must find agreement over the "main things" and be uncompromisingly unified on them going forward.

Preference Issues

Preference issues refer to those everyday matters, big and small, that largely come down to personal inclination. We estimate that at least 90 percent of all marriage decisions fall under this category of issues. Examples include what house to purchase, what color to paint a wall, what food to eat for dinner, and what name to give to each child. Spouses must share input toward these decisions, but they will not always agree. In times of disagreement, seek out ways to serve your spouse by allowing their preference whenever possible.

Poisonous Issues

Poisonous issues include matters of sin, secrecy, and deceit in a marriage. These issues can bring about financial recklessness, sexual infidelity, drug addiction, law-breaking, and a host of other complications. They have the potential to inflict irreparable harm on the entire family. A spouse living in intentional sin might pridefully insist that their toxic actions don't impact anyone else, but their sin has a direct and devastating impact on the other spouse and the entire family. When these reckless behaviors start to happen, you should not sit by and hope they go away. Your silence implies your approval. Instead, you must intervene to make sure the behavior stops as you protect everyone else in the family.

© 2023 by Dave and Ashley Willis, *Married into the Family.* Used by permission. All rights reserved.

All-Time Favorite Marriage Advice

You and your spouse are on the *same team*. It's never him against her or her against him. You're in this together. Since you're on the same team, you'll either win together or lose together. Work together to find solutions through which you'll both win. Fight for and not against each other, and never forget you're on the same team!

This advice might sound too simple to some people, but most of the best marriage advice is really very simple. Humans tend to overcomplicate things and lose sight of that which is clear and plain. We start out instinctively knowing we're in marriage together and on the same team, but then life's stresses and circumstances cloud our vision, and we miss the main point of marriage.

If you are struggling for the unity you once had in your marriage, then call a "team meeting." Apologize to each other and to God. Then create a game plan to get back on the right track. No matter what's been said or done, healing is possible. You can do this! Do not settle for living as strangers, roommates, or rivals. Live as partners, lovers, and best friends.

Return to the team. Start cheering for each other again instead of criticizing. Give each other more high fives and fewer eye rolls. Be willing to apologize for anything you have done to contribute to the current brokenness and be willing to forgive your spouse for their mistakes. Let your words, your actions, and even the tone of your voice communicate this clear message: "I'm with you. I am for you. I love you, and I'll always be on your team."

When it comes to your principles, fight for unity. With issues of preference, celebrate unity within your diversity. As you deal with poisonous issues, demand accountability. In all things, let love lead the way. As you work to craft your family's unified vision and culture, start with love and commitment to God and to each other. When you do this, you will always be heading in the right direction.

© 2023 by Dave and Ashley Willis, *Married into the Family*. Used by permission. All rights reserved.

10 Ways to Make Holidays Fun Again

1. Realize you are not going to please everybody (and that's okay).

2. Try your best to find a balance between how much time you're spending with each family but be sure to give yourselves grace. It will never be exactly even, and that's also okay.

3. Honor your parents but remember that honoring them as married adults doesn't mean obeying them or doing everything they want in the same way you did when you were children. Sometimes you might have to disappoint them in the most honoring, respectful, and loving way you possibly can.

4. Try your best to be fully present wherever you are. Instead of thinking about rushing to the next group of people, focus on relaxing and engaging with the people and activities that are happening right in front of you.

5. Understand that God has called you to be a peacemaker, but not a doormat.

6. If you are traveling and need your own space, don't feel bad about booking a hotel room rather than staying in a family member's home. In fact, this choice might be better for your family too, even though they will not admit it.

7. Make sure you are working to secure moments to connect as a couple even while you try to connect with your relatives.

8. Don't spend money you do not have buying gifts. Stick to a budget and check your motives. Don't use money to try to win favor with your family.

9. Do your best to let your kids experience Christmas morning in your own home. Don't feel bad about establishing your own family holiday traditions.

10. Even amidst the chaos and commercialism that often accompany the holiday season, take time to refocus your mind on what these days are all about: thankfulness, joy, peace, love, and, most of all, Jesus.

© 2023 by Dave and Ashley Willis, *Married into the Family*. Used by permission. All rights reserved.

5 Ways to Build Healthy Bonds

1. Do not treat people the way they treat you; treat people the way God treats you.

The more you love God and embrace His love and grace in your life, the more ability you will have to give love and grace to others. This single principle could transform the way you respond to your in-laws and every other person in your life.

2. Invest in people at strategic low points.

If you want to maximize your positive impact in someone's life, then don't invest in the relationship only when the other person is on top of the world, when they have hit their high points. Give them your best when their stock is low. Serve them when they have no way to repay you. That is real love.

3. Expect nothing in return.

If we only show kindness to those who will return it, then we are not showing love. We're just networking to get ahead. Give your best even when it's not reciprocated. Jesus did that for us, and He calls us to do it for others.

4. Balance tough love with compassion.

When someone we love is in a self-destructive cycle and is a potential harm to themselves or others, we must respond with tough love. Tough love may require an intervention or even legal action, but make sure your motives are always driven by a deep and abiding compassion for the well-being of everyone involved.

5. Don't quit on them, and don't let them quit on themselves.

God calls us to have limitless love for others. This love is not based on our own strength—God's strength is what makes it possible. Once someone realizes that you are going to stick with them no matter what, it can give them the strength to persevere even in difficult circumstances.

© 2023 by Dave and Ashley Willis, *Married into the Family*. Used by permission. All rights reserved.

10 Biblical Character Traits for Healthy In-Law Relationships

1. Respect
Show proper respect to everyone.   —1 Peter 2:17 NIV

2. Generosity
God loves a cheerful giver.   —2 Corinthians 9:7 NIV

3. Humility
God opposes the proud but gives grace to the humble.   —James 4:6

4. Encouragement
Encourage one another and build each other up.   —1 Thessalonians 5:11 NIV

5. Flexibility
I can do all things through Christ who strengthens me.   —Philippians 4:13 NKJV

6. Grace
Be kind and compassionate to one another, forgiving each other, just as in Christ God
forgave you.   —Ephesians 4:32 NIV

7. Gratitude
Give thanks in all circumstances; for this is God's will for you in Christ Jesus.
                                                            —1 Thessalonians 5:18 NIV

8. Hospitality
Always be eager to practice hospitality.   —Romans 12:13

9. Honesty
An honest answer is as sweet as a kiss.   —Proverbs 24:26 NIV

10. Love
Do everything with love.   —1 Corinthians 16:14

© 2023 by Dave and Ashley Willis, *Married into the Family*. Used by permission. All rights reserved.

Changing the Communication

1. Take an inventory of your vocabulary and remove words that are not helpful.

Some unhelpful words are easy for us to spot. Using curse words with your family members obviously has no place, so get rid of profanities, but don't stop there. Also, commit to removing critical words, sarcastic words, or ambiguous words, such as *fine*. These words can do more harm than good. Make sure your words communicate your love and commitment to each other. You should remove from your vocabulary any words that are harming your family.

2. Commit to complete honesty and transparency.

Tell the truth, but always speak it in love. Do not use the truth as a weapon to hurt your in-laws. Speak with tenderness and compassion and never deceit.

3. Learn the difference between discretion and deception.

Sometimes the wisest thing to say is nothing at all. Not every thought that enters your head needs to be shared or said aloud. Certainly, we should err on the side of sharing what is on our hearts, but when the words could be critical or hurtful, the discretion to remain silent and process your thoughts before speaking is the wisest choice. Have the discretion to choose words wisely, but do not ever be deceptive by refusing to confess a sin or by concealing what is really on your heart.

4. Give a lot of grace to your spouse and a lot of grace to yourself too.

Refuse to keep score of each other's faults, and instead, be quick to forgive and seek forgiveness. When you and your family choose to be full of grace, then your relationships with your in-laws can be some of the most enjoyable relationships in your life.

© 2023 by Dave and Ashley Willis, *Married into the Family*. Used by permission. All rights reserved.

Leader Tips for Small Group Use

1. *Plan well but allow the Holy Spirit to change your plans.*
   As members of your group confront issues related to their experiences with in-laws, you may need to take more time than you originally planned. Don't force the group to move on when you need to dig deeper into a particular area.

2. *Create a safe environment.*
   Some group members may need to share some very deep things with the entire group, while others may want to keep their thoughts and feelings more private. Allow room for differences.

3. *Allow time to respond.*
   As you go through the exercises, don't try to answer the questions for the group. Pause when you ask questions. This may seem awkward in the beginning, but it will allow the members of the group time to consider their words carefully.

4. *Listen intently.*
   Don't plan what you are going to say next while members of the group are still talking about an earlier issue. Let the responses of the members shape what you will discuss next. Listen with compassion because some group members will express strong emotions as you go through this book.

5. *Guard your own opinions carefully.*
There is a time to teach and a time to listen. Don't answer your own questions, at least not until everyone else has had an opportunity to respond. If you give your own answers too quickly, then it will stifle the conversation.

6. *Model respect.*
Make sure each person has an opportunity to speak and be heard.

7. *Let prayer be your guide.*
Group members will express many beliefs, opinions, and feelings. Ask God to give you discernment for how to respond to anything that group members express.

8. *Follow up.*
After the session is over, some group members will have more questions and need ongoing attention. Remember, the primary goal is healthy relationships in marriages and families.

Notes

CHAPTER 1. God Speaks About In-Laws

1. Boaz also had a remarkably interesting legacy. His mother was Rahab from Jericho. She was known as a city prostitute, but God saved and redeemed her. Boaz learned generosity and compassion from his heroic mother. You can find Rahab's story in Joshua chapters 2 and 6.

2. In the Bible, a kinsman redeemer was a male relative who could act on behalf of a relative who was in trouble or who needed vindication. In the Torah (the Bible's first five books), there are several laws that apply to the kinsman redeemer. For example, see Leviticus 25:25–28, 47–55; Deuteronomy 25:5–6.

CHAPTER 2. How to Leave & Cleave

1. *Strong's Concordance*, s.v. "1234. Baqa," Bible Hub, accessed April 12, 2023, https://biblehub.com/strongs/hebrew/1234.htm.

2. Ibid.

CHAPTER 3. 10 Unhealthy Types of In-Laws

1. We recognize there are many lists such as these available on the internet and social media. We intentionally avoided looking at or referring to any of these lists as we constructed this chapter. Any similarities are coincidental. We encourage you to explore other Christian resources on in-law dynamics, but we believe we have covered the broad spectrum of unhealthy in-law relationships here.

2. Meaghan Rice, "What Is Narcissistic Gaslighting?" Talk Space Mental Health Conditions, February 7, 2022, https://www.talkspace.com/mental-health/conditions/articles/narcissistic-gas-lighting/.

3. Rice, "What Is Narcissistic Gaslighting?" Stephanie Sarkis, "Are Gaslighters Aware of What They Do?" *Psychology Today* (Sussex Publishers, January 30, 2017), https://www.psychologytoday.com/us/blog/here-there-and-everywhere/201701/are-gaslighters-aware-what-they-do.

4. Sarkis, "Are Gaslighters Aware of What They Do?"

CHAPTER 4. Defining and Setting Boundaries

1. Many good books on healthy boundaries have been written over the last few years, and you can find other good resources online. We recommend Henry Cloud and John Townsend's *Boundaries in Marriage* (Zondervan, 1999).

CHAPTER 6. Difficult Conversations

1. Jimmy Evans, "Successful Communication in Marriage," Sermon presented at Church of the Highlands, (Birmingham, AL: September 25, 2022).

About the Authors

Dave and Ashley Willis spent 13 years in full-time church ministry before devoting their work entirely toward the global mission of building stronger, Christ-centered marriages. Their marriage-related books, blogs, podcast, speaking events, and media resources have reached millions of couples around the world, making Dave and Ashley one of the most recognized and trusted couples in marriage ministry.

They partnered with XO Marriage in 2018. XO Marriage is the nation's largest marriage-focused ministry, and as part of the XO Team, Dave and Ashley speak at all XO events, host the *Naked Marriage* Podcast, and create new marriage resources. Their most recent books include *The Naked Marriage, Naked and Healthy,* and *The Counterfeit Climax.*

Dave holds an MA in communication studies, and Ashley is pursuing an MA in biblical counseling.

The Willis family includes four sons from elementary to college age and a rescue dog. Dave and Ashley loving hanging out with their family, watching movies, and going on long walks, which is also where they develop many of the marriage ministry content ideas.

Marriage Help

We understand that when your marriage is struggling, you need help in a timely manner. XO Marriage is here to support you and stand alongside you in the fight for your marriage. We offer two distinct services:

Coaching on Call
Offered at multiple lengths, these sessions are designed for couples or individuals who are in crisis and need immediate help. Specializing in marital crisis intervention, our team is available to meet you in your time of need to listen with compassion and understanding, provide wise objective counsel, and help you navigate the best plan of action to start the healing process.

Marriage Mediation
Our full day private one-on-one marriage mediation is designed for couples who are struggling with multiple issues and/or feeling hopeless about the future of their marriage. This intensive approach allows couples the extended time needed to fully process their primary issues without the interruption of time or hassle of scheduling multiple weekly sessions.

To learn more, visit **xomarriage.com/help**.

Get exclusive access to the best marriage-building content on any device!

Watch classes, workshops, conferences, and live teachings from leading marriage experts in the comfort of your home.

Start your free trial today, for only $9/month!

xonow.com